The Pronunciation Book

Student-

centred

activities

for

pronunciation

work

**Tim Bowen
and Jonathan Marks**

Pilgrims

Longman

Longman Group UK Limited,
Longman House, Burnt Mill, Harlow,
Essex CM20 2JE, England
and Associated Companies throughout the world.

© **Longman Group UK Limited 1992**

This book is produced in association with Pilgrims Language Courses Limited of Canterbury, England.

First published 1992

Set in 10/12 pt Cheltenham

Produced by Longman Singapore Publishers (Pte) Ltd

Printed in Singapore

British Library Cataloguing in Publication Data
Bowen, Tim
  Pronunciation Book: Student–centred
  Activities for Pronunciation Work. –
  (Pilgrims Longman Resource Books Series)
  I. Title II. Marks, Jonathan III. Series
  428.1
ISBN 0 582 06491 0

Acknowledgements
We are indebted to Longman Group UK Ltd. for permission to reproduce an extract from *Longman Dictionary of Contemporary English* (1978).

We are grateful to the following for their permission to reproduce copyright material:
The Sound Foundations chart on page 5, is copyright, and is reproduced with the permission of Adrian Underhill. Copies of the chart may be obtained from him at International Language Centre, Palace Court, White Rock, Hastings, East Sussex TN34 1JY, United Kingdom.

Illustrations
Cover illustrated by Lara Harwood

Illustrations by Kathy Baxendale

A letter from the Series Editors

Dear Teacher,

This series of teachers' resource books has developed from Pilgrims' involvement in running courses for learners of English and for teachers and teacher trainers.

Our aim is to pass on ideas, techniques and practical activities which we know work in the classroom. Our authors, both Pilgrims teachers and like-minded colleagues in other organisations, present accounts of innovative procedures which will broaden the range of options available to teachers working within communicative and humanistic approaches.

We would be very interested to receive your impressions of the series. If you notice any omissions that we ought to rectify in future editions, or if you think of any interesting variations, please let us know. We will be glad to acknowledge all contributions that we are able to use.

Seth Lindstromberg
Series Editor

Mario Rinvolucri
Series Consultant

Pilgrims Language Courses
Canterbury
Kent
CT1 3HG
England

Tim Bowen

Jonathan Marks

Tim Bowen is a teacher trainer and trainer trainer at ILC, Hastings. He graduated in Russian language and literature from the University of Leeds in 1972, followed post-graduate studies in Czech literature at the University of Brno, Czechoslovakia and took a PGCE course in TEFL at the University College of North Wales. Since then he has taught English and trained teachers in many countries. Tim also regularly leads or co-tutors a variety of teacher training and trainer training workshops on a range of topics from phonology and vocabulary acquisition to teacher development and humanistic approaches. Apart from pre-service and in-service teacher-training, his main interests in language teaching are philology, contrastive linguistics and developing reading skills. He has recently completed an M.Phil thesis on the development of foreign and second language reading skills. Away from TEFL he is a keen linguist, long-distance runner and bibliophile.

Jonathan Marks has worked as a teacher, teacher trainer and trainer trainer mainly at ILC Hastings, and in Germany, Sweden and Poland, but also in other European countries. His main professional interests include pronunciation, teacher development and applications of 'humanistic' approaches. He graduated from Cambridge in English and Modern Languages, and holds an MA TEFL from Reading, a PGCE and the RSA Dip TEFLA. He is a founder member of the IATEFL Phonology SIG, and a frequent workshop and seminar leader and contributor to conferences and other events. With Tim Bowen, he is currently working on a training book for experienced teachers. He is also a member of a team writing a new coursebook series for German-speaking learners of English. He reads, listens to lots of music, goes for long walks, runs a bit, does morris dancing, and likes languages and trains.

Contents

Index of activities

	ACTIVITY	LEVEL	FOCUS
	3.12 Sounds vocabulary game	Elementary +	Pronouncing known vocabulary
	3.13 Sounds anagram race	Elementary +	Recognising sounds; Combining sounds into words
	3.14 Sounds bingo	Beginner +	Recognising sounds
4 SPELLING TO SOUND AND BACK AGAIN	4.1 Sounds maze	Beginner +	Recognising phonemic symbols; Relationships between sounds and spelling
	4.2 Phonemic snap	Beginner +	Relationships between sounds and spelling; Practice in the pronunciation of sounds in words
	4.3 Rhyming sounds	Elementary +	Links between sounds and spelling; Recognising sound/spelling patterns
	4.4 Ongoing vocabulary record	Any	Relationships between pronunciation and spelling
	4.5 Sounds search	Beginner +	Recognising individual sounds and relating sounds to spelling
	4.6 Sounds scrabble	Elementary +	Relationships between sounds and spelling
	4.7 Using sounds for word building	Elementary +	Relationships between sounds and spelling
	4.8 Sounds crosswords	Elementary +	Relationships between sounds and spelling
	4.9 Phonemic word race	Beginner +	Relationships between sounds and spelling
5 SOUNDS IN SEQUENCE	5.1 Assimilation awareness exercise	Elementary +	Awareness of features of connected speech
	5.2 Producing weak forms	Elementary +	Producing weak forms
	5.3 Using listening material	Beginner +	Stressed syllables and weak forms
	5.4 How many words?	Elementary +	Interpreting sounds in fast colloquial speech
	5.5 Connected speech dictation	Elementary +	Sensitising learners to assimilation and elision; Changes in the pronunciation of some words in connected speech
	5.6 Completing limericks	Beginner +	Rhythm, syllable reduction and rhyme
6 WORD STRESS	6.1 Introducing word stress	Beginner +	Introducing the concept of stress
	6.2 Stress patterns	Beginner +	Word stress patterns in English
	6.3 Word stress awareness exercise	Elementary +	Recognising and producing correct stress placement
	6.4 Guess the stress	Any	Predicting word stress
	6.5 Stress matching game	Elementary +	Accurate stress placement
	6.6 Vocabulary revision	Any	Pronunciation as a cue for recalling and categorising vocabulary items
	6.7 Moving stress in phrases	Elementary +	Stress variations according to the position of a word in a phrase
	6.8 Stress in compounds/ two-word expressions	Beginner +	Stress patterns in compounds and two-/ multi-word expressions

	ACTIVITY	LEVEL	FOCUS
7 TONE GROUPS, RHYTHM AND INTONATION	7.1 Tonic prominence recognition exercise	Elementary +	The function of tonic prominence
	7.2 Tonic prominence production exercise	Elementary +	Placing tonic prominence according to intended meaning
	7.3 Twenty questions to a drawing	Elementary +	Contrastive intonation
	7.4 I do	Elementary +	Assigning tonic prominence according to discourse conditions
	7.5 Correct the teacher	Elementary +	Assigning tonic prominence according to discourse conditions
	7.6 Create your own verse form	Lower intermediate +	Rhythmic structures
	7.7 Metronome	Any	Rhythm and compression of unstressed syllables
	7.8 Shadowing	Elementary +	All aspects of pronunciation
	7.9 Video viewing	Elementary +	Awareness of body language as a way into stress and rhythm
	7.10 Pronunciation role play	Elementary +	Differences between the pronunciation of English and that of the mother tongue above the level of individual sounds
8 TROUBLE SHOOTING	8.1 Problems with /w/	Any	Ideas for working on /w/
	8.2 /w/ for /v/	Any	Avoiding /w/
	8.3 /f/ /p/ confusion	Any	Awareness of where the sounds are produced
	8.4 Insertion of /e/ before consonant clusters	Any	Removing intrusive /e/
	8.5 /p/ /b/ confusion	Any	The question of voicing
	8.6 /j/ pronounced as /dʒ/	Any	Using /iː/ to arrive at /j/
	8.7 Initial /h/	Any	Getting louder
	8.8 Intrusive /h/	Any	Through /j/ to /h/
	8.9 Problems with /θ/ and /ð/	Any	Tongue and teeth
	8.10 Dental /t/ and /d/	Any	Moving the tip of the tongue back
	8.11 Intrusive /ə/ in final position	Any	Holding the final fricative
	8.12 Incorrect stress patterns	Any	Awareness of what makes a stressed syllable

Introduction

The Pronunciation Book is aimed at those teachers who wish to incorporate more (or perhaps some) pronunciation work into their general English teaching. It will be of use to all teachers of English who feel the need both to increase their own repertoire of pronunciation teaching techniques and strategies, and to develop their own awareness of and sensitivity towards aspects of English pronunciation. It will be suitable for those teaching different levels of learners from beginner to advanced and will be of use to those teaching younger learners as well as adults. The book will also benefit teachers just entering the profession, as it covers basic areas of sound recognition and production. As such, it will also be a valuable source of teaching material for tutors and participants on teacher training courses (e.g. the RSA/Cambridge Certificate in TEFLA) for both native and non-native speakers alike.

CONTENT

The book includes activities that are based on a number of aspects of pronunciation: sounds, word stress, prominence, aspects of intonation and features of connected speech. These are grouped into eight chapters. The first deals with the basic factors involved in producing sounds and provides a general methodology for the teaching of sounds. The second chapter covers the promotion of awareness of aspects of pronunciation. The third chapter looks at ways in which learners can be helped to acquire and build on their own inventory of sounds. The fourth contains a number of activities designed to promote active awareness of the relationships between sounds and spelling in English. The fifth chapter is concerned with sounds in sequence and the effect on sounds of their environment in continuous speech. The sixth chapter deals with word stress or accent, while the seventh looks at aspects of rhythm and intonation. The final chapter is a 'trouble shooting' chapter, in which possible solutions are suggested for frequently occurring pronunciation problems. This is followed by a glossary of terms used in the book, a pronunciation table, and a short bibliography of books on phonetics and phonology that the authors have found useful.

AIMS

The book is intended simultaneously to heighten teachers' (and learners') awareness of features of English pronunciation and to provide a range of practical classroom activities that teachers can easily incorporate into lessons of all types. The basic aim of the book is to enable teachers to affect their learners' pronunciation in a positive sense in three general ways. Firstly, by increasing the learners' awareness of different aspects of pronunciation. Secondly, by helping them to identify their own particular pronunciation targets in what (without this help) might seem a hopeless and limitless task. Finally, by enabling learners to realise that pronunciation is neither 'dull' nor 'difficult', but that it can be a pleasurable and stress free part of the language learning process.

APPLYING THE ACTIVITIES

The activities and procedures described and illustrated in this book are not intended to be 'pronunciation lessons' in themselves. They could, however, be extended, combined or adapted to form complete pronunciation-based lessons if this seemed appropriate. Rather than complete lessons, they are *pronunciation components* that you can integrate into other lessons. Suggestions are made as to why, where and how you can use the activities and how you can link them to other, non-pronunciation activities. With most of the activities, there are also guidelines for the amount of time a particular activity might normally be expected to take and the materials that you will need. As far as the language level of the learners is concerned, most of the activities can be used at virtually any level from beginner to advanced, although indications of the suitability for particular levels are given at the beginning of each activity.

ORIGINS OF THE BOOK

We have found that many teachers, consciously or unconsciously, avoid teaching pronunciation because they regard it as 'difficult'. But when teachers try out a few simple pronunciation activities of the kind included in this book, they are often surprised at their effectiveness and popularity with learners. We hope that the activities and procedures described in this book will help many more teachers to become more confident when dealing with pronunciation in the classroom, and that the application of these activities and procedures will contribute to a growing awareness of the role and importance of pronunciation in the language learning process as a whole.

Acknowledgements

Thanks are due to Adrian Underhill for his inspirational phonemic chart, to the students of ILC, Hastings, with whom many of the ideas outlined in this book were first tried out, and to the teachers of Jerez de la Frontera, Munich, Stuttgart, Bratislava and Brno for their helpful comments on the activities.

Tim Bowen
Jonathan Marks
April 1992

CHAPTER 1

The basics

1.1 THE PRONUNCIATION TEACHER'S TOOL KIT

The exercises and activities contained in this book require the use of a number of classroom aids. In some cases, these are available commercially, but in others you might find that the simplest solution is to make your own.

We regard the following as essential:

A phonemic chart

This is a chart or table showing the 44 phonemes of the variety of 'standard' British English that is otherwise known as *RP* or *Received Pronunciation*. In corresponding to a standard model (RP), such a chart does not include phonetic variations on the basic 44 phonemes found in various British regional accents and other varieties of English. The type of phonemic chart referred to in this book and used as the basis for many of the activities is *not* intended as a prescriptive model, but rather as a general structural guideline. One way of using a chart based on the 44 phonemes of RP English is to regard the centre of each phoneme square as the 'standard' model, while variations are included around the centre of the square and, in some cases, may even touch the edge of the square and resemble the adjoining phoneme very closely. We are both speakers of non-standard varieties of English and have never found this to be a barrier to using a phonemic chart based on RP or to teaching the sounds it contains!

The 44 phonemes of English are given, with examples of words in which they are found, in most learners' dictionaries. These 44 break down into 12 vowel sounds, 8 diphthongs and 24 consonants. One of the most effective charts as a teaching aid is Adrian Underhill's *Sound Foundations* chart, where the position of the phonemes on the chart is determined by the place and manner of their articulation. A reduced form of this chart is shown on the opposite page for reference purposes. Copies of the chart may be obtained from Adrian Underhill, International Language Centre, Palace Court, White Rock, Hastings, East Sussex, TN34 1JY.

Many teachers like to display a phonemic chart in their classrooms and to use it both to help in the teaching of sounds and to deal with pronunciation problems as they arise. If, for example, a learner pronounces the word 'village' as 'willage', the teacher might point to the phoneme /v/ on the chart, thereby indicating to the learner where the pronunciation error lies. In addition, the chart can function as a 'pronunciation syllabus' for the learners. It provides a visual representation of the sounds of English and can thus help them, with the aid of the teacher, to recognise which sounds they can already produce well and, more importantly, to determine which sounds they need to work on. As such, a phonemic chart is a valuable tool because it can help to provide the learner with a finite goal – the 7 sounds they particularly need to work on, for example.

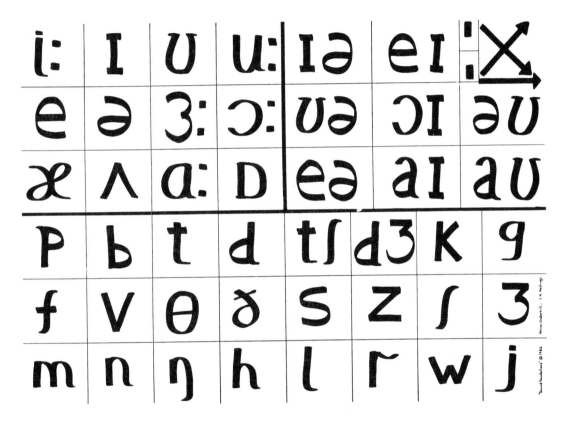

Fig. 1 Sound Foundations chart

Using a phonemic chart presupposes a need on the part of both teachers and learners to learn phonemic script. The advantages of doing so are that phonemic script provides a convenient (and quick) reference point. It is also much more concise than the countless spelling combinations that can represent the sounds of English. It is also a good deal more systematic and accurate than 'homemade' phonetic transcriptions that take the learners' mother tongue as the model for the sounds of English. We have generally found little resistance among learners to using phonemic symbols, although we would suggest that teachers need to be sensitive to problems of overload, particularly at lower levels, with learners whose mother tongue uses non-Roman script. Talking to learners about the importance of good pronunciation and explaining the function of phonemic symbols and the phonemic chart is extremely helpful. When it comes to actually learning phonemic symbols, we have found it particularly important to begin by emphasising the fact that these are symbols representing *sounds* and not letters. /e/, for example, is /e/ as in 'bed' and not /iː/.

We favour a gradual approach, introducing sounds and their symbols as they arise over a series of lessons, rather than presenting all the symbols in a single lesson. We typically introduce up to four sounds in a single lesson, beginning with familiar symbols such as /m/, /s/ and /p/. We also often introduce sounds in contrasting pairs, where we feel the difference in sound quality is particularly important (/iː/ and /ɪ/, for example). We try to consolidate use of the phonemic symbols by quickly contextualising sounds into whole words (/siːt/ and /sɪt/, for example), by giving phonemic transcriptions of new vocabulary items, and by encouraging our learners to use monolingual learners' dictionaries (with consistent phonemic pronunciation guides for each word) and to research the pronunciation of new vocabulary items for themselves. We feel it is essential that the learning and use of the symbols is non-pressurised and that learners should be allowed to acquire the symbols at a pace which suits them, but with a little help from the teacher! Further ideas for exploiting a phonemic chart are contained in section 3.1.

A mouth diagram

Like a phonemic chart, a poster-sized mouth diagram is a convenient and useful teaching aid. You can use it to help your learners identify the parts of the mouth where particular sounds are produced. It is quite difficult to describe the alveolar ridge, for example, and some relatively complex language would be required to do so. Likewise, we do not recommend 'live' demonstrations for this purpose – too messy! A cross-section diagram, with all the major articulatory organs labelled should enable you to refer clearly and simply to these organs whenever necessary. (See Fig. 2 opposite.)

One or more sets of phoneme cards

These are relatively easy to make and form the basis of a number of the activities suggested in this book. You will need several sheets of fairly robust card cut into sets of 44 cards. Each card should be roughly the size of a playing card (approximately 10cm × 7cm). Draw one phonemic symbol on each card using a thick felt tip pen. In the case of /v/ and /ʌ/ and /e/ and /ə/, you will need to indicate, using a small arrow or line, which is the top of the card and which is the bottom.

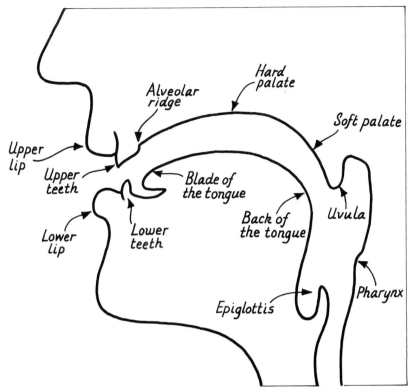

Fig. 2 Mouth diagram
© Longman Group UK Ltd 1992

A tape recorder and some blank tapes

You may find it useful to tape pronunciation listening exercises for your learners. This is particularly important when you wish to have your learners distinguish between vowel sounds, stress patterns or different intonation patterns. Thus, when we say 'Read the sentences aloud ...', you may find it helpful to tape your reading beforehand. There are two big advantages to taping. Firstly, you can provide a constant and consistent model. Secondly, your learners can listen in their own time (perhaps in a self-access centre or language laboratory, or even for homework).

Another role of the tape recorder is to record the learners' own pronunciation. This is a very effective way of giving them feedback on their own performance. If they hear the contrast between a model sentence read by you (or one taken from a coursebook dialogue, for example) and their own version of the sentence, this can help them in a number of ways. It can show them that they still need to improve (an important factor, particularly at higher levels). It can also make them aware of errors in their own performance. In terms of evaluating their own performance, it can also help to encourage and motivate them by making progress evident.

We regard the following as desirable but not essential:

A set of Cuisenaire rods

These are boxes of small wooden bars of different colours and sizes. Their original use was as aids in the teaching of mathematics at junior schools, but many teachers now also use them in language teaching. In teaching pronunciation, the different colours can be used as memory aids to represent different sounds or (see 2.8 *Introducing syllables* and 6.1 *Introducing word stress*) as memory aids to represent different words. If you do not have access to Cuisenaire rods, then some equivalent form of memory aid (such as a set of coloured counters, board magnets or buttons) is a perfectly adequate substitute. (Cuisenaire rods may be obtained from Educational Solutions (UK) Ltd, 11 Crown St, Reading. RG1 2TQ.)

An emphasis pointer

An emphasis pointer is a little like a car aerial – but we do not advise breaking them off as a substitute! We have found the emphasis pointer to be particularly useful when working with a phonemic chart – you point silently to particular symbols and ask learners to produce the corresponding sounds. From the point of view of logistics, a pointer can help you to give your learners a clearer view of the chart as it does not obscure the chart in the same way that an arm does. You can also use one to show rhythm and intonation patterns (in much the same way that a conductor might lead an orchestra), or to point out phonological features (stress, intonation patterns) in example sentences written on the board.

A pocket mirror

A small mirror is useful so that learners can observe their own lip and jaw position when articulating particular sounds (the contrast between /iː/ with spread lips and /uː/ with rounded lips, and /iː/ with jaw almost closed and /æ/ with jaw open, for example).

A metronome

You can use a metronome to provide a completely regular beat in activities practising stressed and unstressed syllables. (See 7.7 *Metronome*.)

TEACHING SOUNDS

You will probably need to help your learners become aware of what happens when they produce sounds in their own language or in English. It is not normally sufficient simply to repeat the sound and expect learners to get it right through hearing alone. Sometimes you will have to show them or explain to them what happens when a particular sound is produced. You will also probably need to show them how to improve their pronunciation of the particular sounds that they are finding difficult. In this section, we are going to address you, the teachers, and suggest that you yourselves follow the steps outlined below. You can then pass the process on to your learners.

What factors do you need to consider?

Vowels and diphthongs

AIR
Say /iː/. Put your hand in front of your mouth. You should feel some (but probably not much) air being expelled from the lungs. Muscle effort is involved in the passage of this air. All vowels require an uninterrupted passage of air, with the tongue and other speech organs affecting the quality of this passage without ever completely blocking it.

VOICING
Whisper /iː/. Place your fingertips lightly on either side of your Adam's apple. Notice the absence of any vibration. Keep your fingertips in position and now utter /iː/ aloud. Notice the vibration. This is *voicing*. Voicing (i.e. the vibration of the vocal cords) is present in the pronunciation of all vowels and diphthongs, as well as some consonants.

JAW
Say /iː/. Notice the position of the jaw. It is probably almost closed. Now say /æ/. Can you feel any difference? Try /iː/ /æ/ /iː/ /æ/ several times in quick succession. You should feel a considerable difference in the jaw position for the two sounds. /iː/ is relatively 'closed', while /æ/ is 'open'. Try the same exercise in pairs and observe the opening and closing of your partner's mouth. If you are working alone, look in a pocket mirror as you repeat the sounds. Next, try the exercise with other combinations of vowel sounds, e.g. /uː/ /ʌ/ and /ɪ/ /ɒ/. Then try with the diphthongs /eɪ/ and /aɪ/. Notice how they begin with the jaw relatively open and end with the jaw closing.

To illustrate the importance of jaw position in the production of vowels and diphthongs, try pronouncing /iː/ with your jaw wide open and /æ/ with your jaw almost closed. It will probably feel very unnatural and difficult to achieve. An even more marked contrast can be achieved by trying to pronounce the diphthong /aɪ/, for example, beginning in a closed position and ending in an open one. You will find that it is virtually impossible to produce anything remotely resembling /aɪ/.

LIPS

Whisper the sound /iː/. Notice the lips. They are spread, almost as if you are smiling (hence the tendency of photographers to ask subjects to say 'cheese' when being photographed). Now say /uː/. You will feel that the lips become rounded, almost as if you are whistling. Try pronouncing /iː/ and then /uː/ several times in rapid succession in pairs and observe the position of your partner's lips and how the position changes from spread to rounded.

To illustrate the importance of lip position, try pronouncing /iː/ with rounded lips. It will probably sound quite different. It may, for example, sound like a French vowel sound. Now try pronouncing /uː/ with spread lips. Notice the difficulty in maintaining the /uː/ sound. Now, preferably working with a partner or with a mirror, notice the lip position for the other vowels. You will see that some tend to be more spread, while others are more rounded. Others still are less pronounced as regards lip position. Next, experiment with the diphthongs and notice how the lip position changes from the starting point to the end of the glide. (For more practice of the above activities see 2.6 *Throwing a phoneme*.)

TONGUE

Pronounce the sound /iː/. Notice the position of the tongue. Is it low in the mouth? Is it flat? You will probably find that it is raised (or 'humped') towards the front of the mouth and is up and making contact with the sides of the front upper molars. Now say /uː/. Again, notice the tongue position. It is probably 'humped' a little further back and is not making such noticeable contact with the roof of the mouth. In fact, it is probably touching the sides of the back upper molars. To feel the contrast more directly, pronounce the sounds /iː/ /uː/ /iː/ /uː/ several times in rapid succession. Notice the movement of the tongue. Now try /ʌ/. Where is the tongue now? Contrast /ʌ/ with /ɔː/. What can you feel? Try the diphthong /ɔɪ/ and notice the movement in tongue position.

LENGTH

What do the following sounds have in common? /iː/, /ɑː/, /ɔː/, /uː/ and /ɜː/? The colon indicates length and suggests that part of the quality of these sounds is that they are longer than certain near equivalents. For example, compare /æ/ and /ɑː/. They are quite clearly different phonemes in English (compare /kæt/ and /kɑːt/) and have a different manner of articulation, but you can still observe the length quality of /ɑː/. Try contrasting it with /æ/ by repeating the contrasting pair several times in rapid succession. Then try the same with /iː/ and /ɪ/, /uː/ and /ʊ/, /ɔː/ and /ɒ/, and /ɜː/ and schwa (i.e. /ə/). You might also try 'shortening' the *long* vowels and 'lengthening' the *short* vowels. Observe what effect this has.

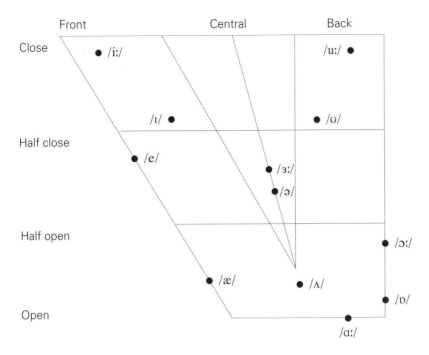

Fig. 3 A diagrammatic representation of the position of English (RP) vowels

Consonants

The production of consonants is affected by a number of factors, but particularly by the manner and place of their articulation. Other factors to consider are the quantity of air flow and the amount of muscle power involved therein, as well as the question of voicing.

MANNER OF ARTICULATION
Prepare to say the sound /p/ but stop just before releasing the sound. Notice that the lips are pressed tightly together and that the passage of air is momentarily obstructed. Now release the sound /p/. You will feel that it is almost like an 'explosion' accompanied by a release of air. Experiment in a similar way with /k/. These sounds are *plosives* (otherwise known as 'stops'). They are characterised by two of the articulatory organs coming together to form a complete closure, blocking the passage of air momentarily. The air is then released to give the plosive sound. There are six plosives in English: /p/, /b/, /t/, /d/, /k/ and /g/.

Now try the sound /f/. Notice how this sound can continue for some time. Unlike the plosives, it is not a single 'explosion' of air. The top teeth and the bottom lip make contact and obstruct the free passage of air, but not completely. There is also a certain amount of friction involved. Now try /s/ and /z/ and notice again the half-obstructed passage of air. These sounds are members of the group known as *fricatives*. The group includes /f/, /v/, /θ/, /ð/, /s/, /z/, /ʃ/, /ʒ/, and /h/. /r/ is also sometimes considered to be a fricative, although it is generally regarded as being frictionless and is often described as a 'frictionless continuant'. Experiment briefly with the sounds /tʃ/ and /dʒ/. Whisper them slowly. Notice how they begin as stops (i.e. there is a complete blockage in the air flow as two of the articulatory organs come together) and continue as fricatives when the stop is released. These two sounds are known as *affricates*.

The phonemes /m/ /n/ and /ŋ/ form a separate group. Practise saying them all several times in rapid succession. You will soon notice that they have a common feature. As with the plosive sounds, there is a blockage in the passage of air somewhere. (In the case of /m/, for example, the lips close to block the air flow.) The air 'escapes' through the nasal cavity, giving all three sounds a nasal quality. These sounds are known, not surprisingly, as *nasals*.

The phoneme /l/ is in a category of its own. Whisper the sound /l/ several times in rapid succession. You will probably notice that the tip or blade of the tongue comes into contact with the ridge behind the teeth (see *Place of articulation* below, for more on this ridge), while the air escapes down both sides of the tongue. This lateral movement of the air flow gives rise to the name of this single-phoneme category, i.e. *lateral*.

Work with a partner. Whisper the sounds /j/ and /w/ several times each in succession but very slowly. Observe your partner's lip positions for each of the sounds. They will probably look very much like the lip positions for the vowel combinations of /iː/ followed by /ə/ and /uː/ followed by /ə/ respectively. As you whisper or mime the sounds, notice your own jaw position. Both sounds will probably begin in a relatively closed position and will open up as you pronounce them. Now experiment by saying the vowel sounds /iː/ and /ə/ together several times, increasing the speed a little each time. After a time, the sound will probably begin to resemble /j/. You can try the same experiment with /uː/ and /ə/ for /w/. Both /j/ and /w/ have a considerable amount of vowel quality and are therefore known as *semi-vowels*.

PLACE OF ARTICULATION

What have /p/, /b/ and /m/ got in common? Mime the words *pan*, *ban* and *man* to a partner in a random order. Your partner will probably have difficulty in telling one from the other. The articulatory organs you are using here are the two lips, hence the term *bilabial* to describe the place of articulation of these three sounds.

Now try /f/ and /v/. Try saying them by pressing down quite hard with the top teeth on the bottom lip. Then try with just a very light contact between the top teeth and the back of the bottom lip. Compare the sounds. To emphasise the role of the teeth in the production of /f/ and /v/, say the sounds /p/ and /f/ alternately several times in rapid succession. You may well find it difficult to do this 'rapidly', but it may also give you some insight into remedies for learners whose mother tongue does not distinguish between /p/ and /f/ and who therefore have problems saying *pull* and *full*, for example. For some light relief, try saying /f/ and /v/ using the bottom teeth and the top lip! Just about possible, but somewhat unusual! The place of articulation of /f/ and /v/ is described as *labiodental*.

What happens with /θ/ and /ð/? Notice that the tip of the tongue comes into contact with the upper teeth. These are described as *dental* sounds. Try saying /t/ and /d/ with the tip of your tongue lightly touching the upper teeth. They will probably sound rather 'soft', as these sounds are not normally dental in English, while in many other languages they are realised as dental sounds.

Just behind your upper teeth you will find a ridge. This is known as the alveolar ridge and a number of English sounds are produced by the tongue coming into contact with the alveolar ridge. Try /t/ and /d/ again and notice the point where the tongue makes contact. Now try /s/, /z/, /l/, /r/ and /n/. Notice where and how the tongue makes contact with the alveolar ridge. In terms of their place of articulation, these sounds are referred to as *alveolar*.

Now try /ʃ/. Where does the tongue make contact? Try contrasting it with /s/ by saying each sound alternately several times. You will feel the tongue 'moving back' for the /ʃ/ sound. Try /ʒ/, /tʃ/ and /dʒ/. Again, it may be useful to contrast them with /s/ or /z/. All four sounds are articulated a little further back from the alveolar ridge, although some contact may be made along the sides. There is contact with the hard palate too. Thus the sounds /ʃ/, /ʒ/, /tʃ/ and /dʒ/ are referred to as *palato-alveolar*.

For the sound /j/, you will notice that the top middle of the tongue is pressing fairly firmly on the sides of the palate. Thus /j/ is known as *palatal*.

The sounds /k/, /g/ and /ŋ/ form a group known as *velar*. Prepare to say /k/, but do not articulate it. Notice where the stop is formed. It will probably feel as if it is somewhere at the back of the mouth. It may even feel a bit uncomfortable. If you have problems locating it, then try /p/ and /k/ alternately several times in quick succession. The /k/ stop is formed by the back of the tongue coming into contact with the soft palate, or velum, hence *velar*.

Finally, we have the sound /h/. Try whispering it 'aloud' with as much air as possible. Try this several times in rapid succession. It will probably create the effect of panting as if out of breath. The point of contact at the onset of the fricative will probably seem to be some-where deep in the throat. There is normally some contact at the glottis and the place of articulation is thus referred to as *glottal*.

VOICING

As with vowels, voicing (or, in this case, the absence of voicing too) is an important factor with consonants. For a simple experiment, place the fingertips lightly on either side of your throat or put your fingers in your ears, pronounce the sound /f/ and hold it for some time. Change to /v/ and hold this sound. You will now notice some vibration. Alternate rapidly between /f/ and /v/. Notice how the vibration stops and starts – /v/ is voiced but /f/ is voiceless. Most consonants are voiced (i.e. accompanied by vibration of the vocal cords) but eight are not: /p/, /t/, /tʃ/, /k/, /f/, /θ/, /s/ and /ʃ/.

FORTIS AND LENIS

If there is no voicing when the voiceless consonants above are pronounced, how is it that we hear them at all? A simple experiment with a sheet of paper should demonstrate the essential quality of the voiceless consonants. Hold the sheet about nine centimetres in front of your face with the bottom of the sheet at approximately the level of your chin. Say the sound /b/ several times. Now switch to /p/. This time, the sheet of paper will normally move quite noticeably. Thus a large amount of air (*fortis*) is released in the pronunciation of the voiceless consonant /p/ and hardly any (*lenis*) in its voiced equivalent /b/. The same phenomenon can be observed with all the voiceless consonants.

Please note that we are not suggesting that learners need to know these 'technical' terms. Nor are we suggesting that you need to know them either. We do, however, feel that it is important for teachers to know basically what goes on when sounds are produced. If you have some idea of how and where a particular sound is produced, then you have some chance of being able to affect the learner's production of that sound by other means than simply asking them to repeat it after you. In that respect, some of the words used above *are* important, e.g. *teeth*, *tip of the tongue*, *air flow*, *voice*, *vibration*. Many of these can be demonstrated and will gradually be picked up by your learners through use. Others can be shown on a mouth diagram (see page 7).

1.3 PRONUNCIATION IN DICTIONARIES

Perhaps the most obvious use of dictionaries in foreign language learning is as a way of accessing meanings of words, in the form of translations or definitions. But dictionaries have many other uses. Among other things, they are a valuable source of information about the pronunciation of words.

You can encourage learners to check pronunciations in the classroom by using their dictionaries. When the habit is established and the learners are familiar with the conventions used, they will be able to make use of this resource whenever they need it, in or out of the classroom. At the same time, however, looking in the dictionary need not be the first step. Learners can be encouraged first to predict the pronunciation of problematic words, and then to use the dictionary as a checking device. The combination of these two approaches is a valuable contribution towards making learners independent in their dealings with English pronunciation.

Most dictionaries, especially those specifically intended for learners' use, show word stress by small superscript marks, and show the sequence of sounds in a word by a selection of symbols from the International Phonetic Alphabet. The exact conventions vary somewhat from one dictionary to another, but the divergences from a system which is already familiar are easy to learn. Most dictionaries also offer some information about variations in pronunciation; the greatest detail is given in specialised dictionaries of pronunciation such as the *Longman Pronunciation Dictionary* (Wells, 1990).

OPPORTUNITIES FOR PRONUNCIATION WORK IN GRAMMATICALLY AND FUNCTIONALLY ORIENTATED LESSONS

1.4

LEVEL
Any

FOCUS
Attention to pronunciation in non-pronunciation orientated lessons

This is a general procedure for integrating a phonological perspective into other classroom work. Although it is often useful to isolate particular elements of pronunciation and devote activities specifically to them, it is also worth remembering that every lesson, unless it is a completely silent one (and maybe even then!), is to some extent a pronunciation lesson, even though the main focus may be on something else. Furthermore, in a lesson which gives high priority to oral accuracy in the use of certain constructions, the learners' pronunciation may contribute to or detract from the achievement of optimal accuracy.

Preparation

Take key examples of the grammatical or functional items you want the learners to practise in the lesson and, alongside your preparation for illustrating the meaning and giving relevant practice opportunities, think of how the examples should be said, paying attention to naturalness and appropriacy to context. Identify likely points of pronunciation difficulty and plan ways of helping learners with these. Here is a suggested checklist of aspects of pronunciation which may prove relevant to particular language points:

- segmentation
- weak forms
- rhythm
- word stress
- linking
- sounds
- intonation
- sound sequences

Procedure

At the point in the lesson when the learners begin to use examples of the new construction, monitor their performance carefully. Listen both for accuracy in assembling the right words in the right order and for accuracy of pronunciation. Correct and give help as necessary so that the learners' performance becomes as good as possible. Refer back to these corrections and improvements on subsequent occasions, in the same lesson or later, when the same constructions are being practised in a controlled way. For example:

If I'd known *you* were coming, I'd have stayed at home.

Learners often find sentences of this type difficult because of the conceptual task of remembering the assembly instructions for the bits and pieces of verb. But such sentences are also quite daunting in terms of pronunciation, and giving due attention here can help confidence greatly. In the example sentence above, assistance in the following areas would be possible:

■ segmentation: two parts, with a more or less clearly audible break between them, often indicated in writing by a comma
■ rhythm: ooOOooo ooOoO
■ linking: 'you‿were', 'I'd‿have' with no /h/
■ intonation: probably ↘↗ on 'you were coming', ↘ on 'home'
■ weak forms: 'I'd' rather than 'I had', /wə/ for 'were', 'I'd' rather than 'I would', /əv/ for 'have', /ət/ for 'at'
■ word stress: not much of a problem here
■ sounds: depends on the learners – maybe the diphthong in 'known', maybe the -*ng* in 'coming'
■ sound sequences: depends on the learners – maybe the sequence /fst/ in 'have stayed'.

1.5 USING DIALOGUES

Reading dialogues out loud is an age-old procedure in foreign language teaching and learning. It can easily suffer from the drawback that the reading is mumbled, stilted, lacking in confidence, and reveals little understanding of the content or of its communicative purpose. Confidence and quality of production can be helped by:

■ giving or eliciting plenty of information about setting and role, so that the dialogue activity takes on something of the quality of a role play
■ allowing plenty of practice time, during which you monitor and help out with any pronunciation difficulties
■ encouraging the readers not to keep their eyes glued to their text, but to imagine they are rehearsing a scene in a film and to look at their interlocutor, safe in the knowledge that the text is there to refer to if they need it
■ getting them to act out the scene instead of just sitting in their seats.

With a sufficiently motivated class, dialogues can be recorded on video or audio tape for analysis of strengths and weaknesses and perhaps further practice and recording. Work on pronunciation, and indeed on language learning as a whole, is helped if the learners are willing to speak out loudly and clearly instead of mumbling uncertainly. For a lot of people, this is easier to begin to do if there is a role to play and a predetermined script to follow.

USING WRITTEN TEXTS

1.6

LEVEL
Elementary +

FOCUS
Relationships between spoken and written forms of English

MATERIALS
Copies of the text or an overhead transparency

TIME
Variable

This activity can be a main lesson activity in its own right or can act as a quick consolidation of certain features of pronunciation using a text which has already been used for other purposes (in the same lesson or at some earlier time). It also works well as a prelude to other types of work using the same text.

Preparation

Make copies of the text if necessary. Do the activity that you are going to ask the class to do, and note your answers for reference. Any short piece of written English will be suitable as a text, but particularly something which is in some way already familiar to the learners. For example, a passage from a reader or coursebook; a text which they have used to work on reading, vocabulary, or grammar; an extract from something they have written themselves.

Procedure

This is actually a group of sub-activities, any number of which can be done at any one time. Any of them could be made into a predictive exercise before listening to a spoken or recorded version of the text. However, it is important for everyone to realise that there is often not simply one correct predicted answer. This is especially true of the sub-activities on connected speech and intonation (8–12 below). All of these sub-activities can involve either the entire text, one paragraph, or just one sentence.

1 Learners find how many times a certain phoneme (or 'sound') occurs. If the class are familiar with phonemic symbols, use them; if not, give an oral model of the sound, and possibly some exemplifying words from outside the text. For example, *eye, night, right, why, like* all contain instances of /aɪ/. This knowledge gives them an informal clue about what to search for.

2 They find how many different spellings there are for a certain phoneme. For example, in the above list, there are four different spellings of /aɪ/.

3 They find how many different phonemes are represented by a certain spelling. For example, the *o* in 'box' represents /ɒ/; the *o* in 'close' represents /əʊ/; the *o* in 'proceed' represents /ə/.

4 They find how many different phonemes (or only vowels, or only consonants) are represented in the text.

5 They find how many phonemes (or only vowels, or only consonants) are *not* represented in the text.

6 They find how many words there are with three syllables (or one, or two, or four ...).

7 They find how many words there are with a certain stress pattern. For example, *important, instruction, complaining* all have the pattern oOo (three syllables with the stress on the second).

8 They find examples of weak forms. For example, *are* and *to* in 'What are they going to do?'

9 They find potential examples of elision. For example, interesting → intresting, West Bank → Wes Bank.

10 They find potential examples of assimilation. For example, *followed by* → /fɒləʊbbaɪ/, *Green Park* → /griːmpɑːk/.

11 They find potential examples of linking. For example, *high up* (linking /j/), *do one* (linking /w/), *fair answer* (linking /r/).

12 They predict how they would divide a sentence into tone groups, where the main prominences would be, and what the intonation patterns would be.

CHAPTER 2

The beginnings of awareness

PRONUNCIATION QUESTIONNAIRE

Before learners embark on any serious pronunciation work, it is a good idea to let them air their own views and understanding of what the task of pronunciation learning entails, and what their personal aims are. Of course, these may well change with time, and the questions suggested here could usefully be returned to at a later stage.

Preparation

Copy the questions onto an A4 master sheet. You might want to change or add to the ones given here. Make a class set.

What does 'pronunciation' include?
How have you learned English pronunciation so far?
What have you found easy/difficult?
What are the main differences between the pronunciation of English and that of your language?
How important do you think pronunciation is? Why?
How well would you like to pronounce English?
What can you do to improve your pronunciation?

© Longman Group UK Ltd 1992

Procedure

1 Hand out the questions to groups of learners and let them think and talk about them for a few minutes.
2 Give them a chance to report back to the whole class and compare views.

VARIATION
In a monolingual class at a very elementary level, it would be preferable to give the questions in the mother tongue.

2.1

LEVEL
Any

FOCUS
Awareness of the scope and importance of pronunciation

MATERIALS
A class set of questionnaire handouts

TIME
10–40 minutes

2.2

LEVEL
Pre-beginner

FOCUS
Awareness of
general features of
English
pronunciation

MATERIALS
A radio which can
receive broad-
casts in a variety
of languages
(short wave is
good) or a
recording made
by switching
between stations

TIME
5 minutes +

RADIO DIAL

Procedure

1 Switch on the radio (or start the recording) and tune in to any station. Ask the class to say whether or not they think the language being spoken is English.

2 Move to another station, and another, and so on, repeating the procedure. When the class hear a language they think is English, ask them why they think so. Of course, one reason might be that they recognise some words. But they will probably also comment on the overall sound of the language. Get them to be as explicit as possible about this. What is it exactly that they recognise as 'Englishness'? They may even be able to imitate the sound of the language, including characteristic phonemes, rhythms and intonation patterns.

RATIONALE

The idea of this activity is to tune in to the overall sound of English even at the stage where the learners cannot yet identify many words. In fact, identifying words and listening for understanding can be a distraction from the task in hand.

2.3

LEVEL
Beginner +

FOCUS
Sensitising
learners to
differences in the
sound of their
mother tongue
and English

MATERIALS
A list of words or
names common to
both English and
the mother tongue
of the learners

TIME
Variable

COMPARING SOUNDS

You can use this simple activity to focus your learners' attention on features of English pronunciation that are markedly different from their mother tongue. The activity works by comparing the pronunciation of words that may be written in the same way in both the mother tongue of the learners and in English, but are pronounced in quite a different way, for example, *situation* in French and English. (Note that the meaning of such words is not important to the exercise, so if the meaning differs in the two languages, this will not affect the aims of the activity.) If a given mother tongue does not share enough common words with English, or if you have a multilingual class, use place names or the names of famous people. In a multilingual class, this can give rise to some interesting comparisons!

Procedure

1 Divide the learners into pairs.

2 Give each pair a copy of the word list (see example opposite).

3 Tell the learners that all the words have one thing in common, they are all pronounced differently in English from the way they are pronounced in their mother tongue.

4 Let each pair experiment (simultaneously) for a few minutes with the possible English pronunciation of the familiar words.
5 Get suggestions from the class as to how the English versions are pronounced. Give a correct model where necessary.
6 Compare the mother tongue pronunciation with the English pronunciation. Draw attention to where the differences lie. For example, in the French and English pronunciations of *Paris*, you could point out the different word stress, silent final 's' in the French version, different vowel sounds in the second syllable, different pronunciation of 'r'. Thus, a single word can reveal a number of interesting comparisons.

Example mother tongue/English word list

Madrid	Paris	Los Angeles	Thatcher
Chicago	Luxembourg	Brazil	Edinburgh
America	Europe	Australia	Barcelona
Shakespeare	Avis	Heathrow	Japan

© Longman Group UK Ltd 1992

BILINGUAL MINIMAL PAIRS

2.4

LEVEL
Any

FOCUS
Awareness of what is involved in learning the accent of a foreign language

MATERIALS
A list of *minimal pairs*, each pair comprising words from English and the mother tongue which have more or less the same pronunciation

TIME
10 minutes +

REQUIREMENT
You must be able to pronounce both languages well

This activity is most obviously suited to monolingual classes, making use of contrasts between English and the mother tongue. However, it can also be used with multilingual classes, using one mother tongue or a mixture, and the point will still be made in a more general way.

Procedure

1 Put up on the board or OHP the list of minimal pairs. The example below is for German/English.

Vieh	fee	hier	here
putz	puts	Ei	eye
Schuh	shoe	Beule	boiler
denn	den	oder	odour
Föhn	fern	hau	how
vor	four	Bild	build
kann	can	Neuß	noise
Ahr	are	drei	dry
Gott	got		

© Longman Group UK Ltd 1992

2 Tell the learners you are going to read down the list, but choosing only one word from each pair, either in English or the mother tongue. Ask them to identify which choice you have made in each case, by shouting out the language (in this case, 'English!' or 'German!').
3 Ask them to reflect on how they identified which language was being spoken. The discussion may well begin with generalities such as 'They sounded different' or 'Language X is softer, or clearer, or more

musical', etc. This is fine as a starting point, but ask the learners to focus more on what was happening in the speaker's speech organs that was different for the two languages.

VARIATIONS

1 If you think it necessary, go through the preliminary stage of reading down the list saying both words in each pair, giving the learners a chance to hear the differences before they have to identify them.

2 Use international words which are pronounced more or less the same in the two languages. For example, in many languages, *restaurant*, *bank*, *telephone*, *computer* are pronounced in roughly the same way.

RATIONALE

This is a way of encouraging learners to investigate exactly what they need to do in order to speak with a native-like accent. (Of course, whether or not they want to aim for this must be their choice.) Rather than concentrating on particular phonemes, it invites them to consider more general features of articulatory setting in different languages, i.e. the typical distribution of muscular tension and movements of the speech organs which constitute the accent of a language.

They can rehearse, perhaps on their own, both members of some of the minimal pairs, and can notice what differences occur in their movements of articulation and the corresponding sound produced. Possible differences (of course they will vary according to the languages in question) include:

- Completely different articulation of corresponding sounds. (For example, *r* in 'dry' and 'drei'.)
- Possibilities of occurrence which exist in one language but not the other. (For example, in the list above, voiced plosives and fricatives in word final position in English but not in German.)
- More or less tension in the neck, jaws, lips or tongue.
- More or less tension generally.
- More or less active use of the larynx.
- Frequent contact between the tongue and the back of the top teeth, or between the tongue and the alveolar ridge.
- Differences of vowel length.
- Differences of consonant length.
- Differences in degrees of lip-rounding.
- More or less tendency for vowels to be diphthongised.

All such information contributes towards a precise specification of the task of pronouncing a language in a native-like way.

Some of the pairs given in the sample list above share the same meaning, but most of them do not. Either way it does not matter; the exercise is concerned with pronunciation, not meaning.

ACKNOWLEDGEMENT

It was Bryan Jenner who led us to think in a more principled way about what accents are and how they differ.

FINDING MISSING VOWELS

English has lots of different vowel sounds, and the task of learning to pronounce them all can seem daunting. Here, we suggest a simple strategy which uses vowels that the learners can already produce for discovering the articulation of ones they can't. For example, the learners can pronounce /iː/ (as in *beat*) and /uː/ (as in *boot*) reasonably well, but not /ɪ/ (as in *bit*).

Procedure

1 Ask the learners to pronounce /iː/, then /uː/, then a continuous sound that slides from /iː/ to /uː/. If they haven't done this before, it might take a bit of practice. Get them to stretch the sound over ten seconds or so.

2 What they need to do now is practise starting the same slide, but stop part-way along, isolating the sound they are making and pronouncing it without unnatural lengthening. If it sounds too much like /uː/, they need to go back; if it sounds too much like /iː/, they need to go further. With trial and error, they should be able to stop at the point where the slide passes through /ɪ/.

3 They will be able to use this strategy, as long as they need to, to rediscover the sound. They can then put the newly-discovered sound to work in words and more ambitious structures.

EXTENSION
They can learn to pronounce not only other pure vowels, but diphthongs using the same strategy. For example, /eɪ/ is a glide from /e/ to /ɪ/.

RATIONALE
The vowels of any variety of English are only a small selection from the innumerable ones which any human voice can make. Learning new vowel sounds can be facilitated by relating them, in the geography of the mouth, to familiar ones, either in English or in the mother tongue. The geographical relationships between the English vowels are indicated in a simplified form in the *Sound Foundations* chart (page 5). For instance, the glide from /iː/ to /uː/ passes through /ɪ/, and a glide from /uː/ to /ɒ/ passes through /ɔː/. Therefore /ɔː/ can be found by stopping part-way along the glide; equally, /ɒ/ can be found by extending the /uː/ to /ɔː/ glide.

2.5

LEVEL
Any

FOCUS
Articulating new vowels

MATERIALS
None

TIME
5 minutes +

2.6

LEVEL
Beginner +

FOCUS
Producing sounds

MATERIALS
None

TIME
10–15 minutes

THROWING A PHONEME

You can use this exercise either as a warmer or as a part of a lesson devoted to improving pronunciation. The exercise reveals the importance of lip position in the production of phonemes, particularly vowels and diphthongs.

Procedure

1 Ask the learners to sit in a circle.
2 Sit in the circle yourself and start the activity by silently miming a phoneme and 'throwing' it to one of the learners in the circle.
3 The learner vocalises the sound which has been thrown. If they do so correctly, then it is their turn to continue by silently miming another phoneme and throwing it to another learner. If not, throw the same phoneme to another learner in the circle, and so on until someone gets it right.
4 Continue for as long as seems profitable. Errors are part of the fun!

2.7

LEVEL
Any

FOCUS
Recognising and producing long vowel sounds; Developing confidence and group trust; Lowering inhibitions

MATERIALS
None

TIME
5–10 minutes

VOWEL CHANTING

Procedure

1 The class stand in pairs, A and B, spread around the room.
2 Student A chooses one of the five long vowel sounds (/iː/, /uː/, /ɑː/, /ɔː/, /ɜː/) and chants it to B, who listens with eyes closed, paying close attention to the quality of the vowel and of A's voice.
3 B closes her eyes again. A moves to another part of the room, and guides B towards him by chanting the same vowel as before. B has to home in on A's voice amidst all the chanting of the other members of the class.
4 A and B change roles.
5 A and B change partners.

VARIATION
Everyone in the class uses the same vowel sound.

ACKNOWLEDGEMENT
We learnt this from Adrian Underhill, who adapted it from a Mongolian chanting technique.

INTRODUCING SYLLABLES

Understanding what a syllable is is an important precondition for work on stress. Here is the way of establishing that understanding using a non-intellectual, guided discovery approach. The usefulness of this exercise will be particularly clear to learners if it is closely followed by the *Introducing word stress* activity (6.1) and the introduction or remedial treatment of some vocabulary in which a number of syllables and/or stress placements are problematic.

Procedure

1 Invite learners, one by one, to suggest English words – perhaps words they particularly like, or which they have recently learnt. Without giving any explanation, represent each word by laying a rod (or equivalent) on the table, so that words with the same number of syllables are clustered in different areas of the table (see Fig. 4 below).

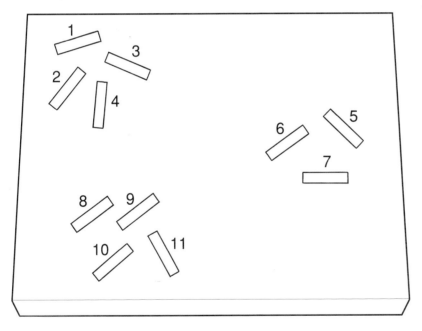

1 Monday	5 now	8 Saturday
2 always	6 got	9 Nottingham
3 Wednesday	7 week	10 beginning
4 sitting		11 important

Fig. 4 Groups of Cuisenaire rods showing the number of syllables in different words

2.8

LEVEL
Most suitable for near-beginners, but may be needed at any level

FOCUS
Introducing the concept of the syllable

MATERIALS
A table; Some Cuisenaire rods or similar (see page 8)

TIME
10–15 minutes

Each area of the table becomes the domain of words with a certain number of syllables, and each word is associated with its position on the table, its length and the colour of the rod representing it. Proceed slowly, pausing after the addition of each new word to allow the class to take in the scene, and pointing frequently at the rods to elicit recall of the words.

2 After a while, when there are a good few rods on the table, let the class begin trying to put rods into the appropriate group to represent new words which are suggested. If it seems that no one is going to catch on, prompt them by saying some of the words already on the table and simultaneously tapping the number of syllables. More likely, some of the class will get the idea and try to explain to the others by counting or tapping or perhaps by using the word *syllable* or its mother tongue equivalent. Continue with the same procedure for a while, ensuring that some responses are made by learners who initially seemed unsure. Suggest words yourself and get the class to locate them correctly.

3 Finally, using the example words on the table, you can introduce language such as:

Saturday has got three syllables.
How many syllables has it got?
How many syllables are there in this word?

This can then become part of the working language of the classroom.

CHAPTER 3

Learning the inventory of sounds

EXPLOITING THE PHONEMIC CHART

You will find that a phonemic chart is a useful teaching aid. If you display one in your classroom, you can refer to it when pronunciation problems occur. You can also use it to elicit the pronunciation of a particular sound or word and to correct pronunciation errors.

Procedure

1 Begin by pointing to familiar symbols, i.e. symbols which are either identical to, or closely resemble the equivalent letter of the alphabet. Examples are: /m/, /n/, /p/, /b/, /r/, /l/, /w/, /h/, /s/, /z/, /t/, /d/, /k/, /g/, /f/, /v/ and /e/.
2 Gradually introduce other sounds. As a rough rule of thumb, introducing about four new sounds per lesson is probably enough.
3 Point to the new sound on the chart, for example, /iː/. Give a clear model and then ask the learners to repeat. Pay particular attention to both length and lip position in the case of vowels.
4 Now place the sound in context by making a word or a series of words, pointing to the appropriate phonemic symbols, for example, /miːt/, /piːt/, /siːt/, /pliːz/, and so on. Ask the learners to repeat the words as you point to the sounds.
5 As you introduce more sounds you can invite learners to come out to the chart and point first to sounds and then to words that you call out. Later, you can ask learners themselves to call out words.

It should be emphasised at this point that this is a relatively slow process. It takes quite a long time for many learners to assimilate the symbols and to recognise and produce the sounds they represent. Our own preference is to introduce the sounds gradually over a series of lessons, in relatively short lesson sections, without any pressure on the learners to learn the symbols. We also refer to the chart when appropriate in the course of various types of non-pronunciation based activities such as a vocabulary-based lesson, so that the learners become accustomed to the chart being used as an integral part of every lesson. There may be learners who question its use. In such cases, we have found it useful to point out the benefits of being able to work out the pronunciation of new

3.1

LEVEL
Beginner +

FOCUS
Familiarising learners with the content and layout of the phonemic chart

MATERIALS
Phonemic chart (see page 5)

TIME
Variable

vocabulary items on the basis of the phonemic transcriptions given in dictionaries and the value of knowing the symbols to this end.

Learning more about the chart

6 Ask the learners to suggest why the chart is divided into three sections.

7 Having established that these three sections are vowels, diphthongs and consonants, ask the learners why they think the vowels are ordered as they are. You can help here by asking why /iː/ is at the top and /æ/ at the bottom, and why /iː/ is at the front and /uː/ at the back.

8 Give them time to discuss these questions in pairs or small groups.

9 Establish the principles of open and closed vowels (jaw position) and front and back vowels (tongue position). Ask them to produce contrasting sounds (e.g. /iː/ and /uː/, and /iː/ and /æ/) and *feel* the difference in jaw and tongue position.

10 Ask the learners to observe the position of your lips as you pronounce /iː/ and /uː/ respectively. Invite them to try to produce /iː/ with rounded lips and /uː/ with spread lips. The resultant strange noises usually illustrate the importance of lip position very effectively!

11 Ask the learners to suggest why the first two lines of consonants are in pairs (e.g. /p/ and /b/, /t/ and /d/).

12 Establish the principle of voiceless and voiced consonants. /s/ and /z/ are good examples for this purpose. You can ask the learners to place their fingertips lightly on their throat (roughly in the location of the Adam's apple) and pronounce /s/ and then /z/. Ask them if they can feel any difference. The vibration produced by /z/ as opposed to /s/ is usually very striking. You can also ask them how /s/ can be heard if there is no vibration. Placing the palm of the hand in front of the mouth and then pronouncing /z/ and /s/ respectively should clearly illustrate that more air is exhaled in the production of /s/. You can use similar procedures with other pairs of voiced and voiceless consonants, although the fricatives work best because they can be continued for a certain length of time unlike stops such as /p/ and /b/.

EXTENSION

One idea that we have found effective is to give learners their own personal 'mini-copy' of the phonemic chart and to ask them to shade in the phonemes that they can produce relatively accurately. (They will normally need your help to do this.) The unshaded phonemes are the ones they still need to work on. In most cases, there will not be very many of these, typically no more than ten. The effect of this exercise is to focus learners on exactly which phonemes are problematic and to give each learner a finite goal in what might otherwise seem to be an enormous and unidentifiable task.

You might find it helpful to refer to *Learner English* (Swan and Smith, 1987) or *Teaching English Pronunciation* (Kenworthy, 1987) for examples of typical phonemic differences between English and a number of major world languages.

PHONEME EXCHANGE

Procedure

1 Give each learner a phoneme card. Tell them not to show it to the other learners.
2 Go to each learner in turn and check that they can pronounce the sound on their card adequately.
3 Ask all the learners to stand up. This is a mingling activity!
4 Each learner finds a partner and says their sound out loud to them (more than once if necessary). The other learner says their own sound out loud to the first learner. The two learners then exchange cards and say the sound on their new card. Note that all the learners should be working simultaneously.
5 The activity continues until all the learners have attempted all of the sounds. They may, of course, receive the same card more than once.
6 Stop the activity at any time and ask the learners to pronounce the sound they now have on their card. Compare this with the pronunciation at the beginning of the activity.

3.2

LEVEL
Beginner +

FOCUS
Warming up;
Pronouncing
phonemic
symbols

MATERIALS
One set of
phoneme cards

TIME
5–10 minutes

USER-FRIENDLY TONGUE TWISTERS

Preparation

You need a sentence with frequent occurrence of a sound which is problematic for your learners, or two sounds which they tend to confuse. For example:

/θ/ and /ð/:
The thought of another Thursday like the last three didn't exactly thrill Theodore's mother.

/ɔː/ and /ɜː/:
Early morning workers walking to work.

It is certainly possible to use well-known tongue twisters to provide practice of difficult sounds and sound contrasts (e.g. 'She sells sea shells on the sea shore' for distinguishing between /s/ and /ʃ/). If learners find these at all manageable, they can be very useful. However, the whole point of tongue twisters is that they are tricky even for native speakers. The idea that we present here is to provide short, easily-

3.3

LEVEL
Any

FOCUS
Producing difficult
sounds

MATERIALS
Practice
sentences – see
Preparation

TIME
Variable

memorised practice material which does not go out of its way to be as difficult as possible, but contains a high frequency of a certain sound, or sounds. This material can be used in the classroom and also offered as takeaway pronunciation practice.

Procedure

Learners practise individual words, then phrases, then the complete sentence with natural speed and rhythm.

VARIATION
Get them to write tongue twisters for themselves and each other to practise. It may well turn out that these are less likely to be beyond their productive capacity than those devised by native speakers.

3.4

LEVEL
Any

FOCUS
/h/

MATERIALS
A list of learners' utterances involving missing or mispronounced /h/ – 'Can you 'elp me?', 'I don't know 'ow to spell it.'

TIME
5–10 minutes

/h/ THROUGH WHISPERING

/h/ is commonly either omitted (for example, by many native speakers of French and Italian) or replaced by a velar fricative (for example, by many native speakers of Spanish and Russian). Although this is un-likely to lead to any real misunderstanding, it is important because many speakers of English seem to attach a high value to the correct use of /h/, and learners may get a friendlier reception in some quarters if they are able to achieve this.

Procedure

1 Ask the learners to practise whispering, to themselves or to a partner, just to get them used to the idea. It may be useful to suggest a topic for them to whisper about, or, at low levels, a text to read.
2 They then practise whispering the following words, loudly and forcefully.

heat	hill	hurt
who	help	happy
husband	hard	hot
hear	hair	hay
high	whole	how

© Longman Group UK Ltd 1992

The vocabulary used may vary to suit the class, but choose words like those above with a variety of vowel sounds following the /h/.
3 Ask learners to say these words very slowly, starting each word in a whisper but switching the voice on (or switching the whisper off) during the vowel sound, without pausing. For example, heeeeee(*whispered*)eeeeeat(*normally*). Note that it is easiest to stretch words with long vowels.
4 Finally, ask them to repeat this procedure, but to gradually speed up until they are saying the words at normal speed.

5 The words practised can be put into phrases and sentences for further practice, and you can feed other /h/ words in. Be careful not to ask the learners to pronounce /h/ in unstressed words like the *he* of 'Is he there?' where the/h/ is not normally pronounced.

RATIONALE

This procedure is based on the fact that /h/ can be regarded not only as an independent sound, but as a voiceless onset to the following vowel. Whispering is speaking without voicing. (See 8.7 and 8.8 for techniques to overcome other problems with /h/.)

TEST THE TEACHER

3.5

This is a variation on the use of minimal pairs which turns the tables and allows the learners to test the teacher. The same procedure can be applied to word stress patterns, intonation, rhythmic patterns in sentences. For this imaginary class, the contrasting sounds are /əʊ/ and /ɔ:/, and the list might be:

oh	or
so	saw
low	law
coal	call
coat	caught
boat	bought

© Longman Group UK Ltd 1992

Procedure

1 Write the list on the board as above.
2 Invite learners, one by one, to say any one of the words on the board. Say that you will point to the word you hear, and they should say 'Yes' if that was the word they said and 'No' if it wasn't.
3 Point silently to the word you hear, preferably with a pointer rather than your finger. If you aren't sure whether you have heard, for example, *coat* or *caught*, point in between the two. If you hear something different, like *curt* for instance, point somewhere else on the board.
4 If one of the learners says 'No' to your response, either give them more time straight away to try to refine their intended pronunciation, or let them wait a while until they are ready.

VARIATION

Instead of just a two-way sound contrast, you could use three or four confusing sounds for this activity.

RATIONALE

The learners are in control and the teacher gets the 'No' for being wrong, which makes it, at least for many learners, a fairly risk-free and enjoyable way of trying out the accuracy of their pronunciation.

LEVEL
Any

FOCUS
Could be any aspect of pronunciation. This example is concerned with sound contrasts

MATERIALS
A list of minimal pairs containing sounds that your class confuse

3.6

LEVEL
Any

FOCUS
Producing the 'missing' member of a voiced/voiceless fricative pair

MATERIALS
None

TIME
A couple of minutes whenever needed, for example, in connection with vocabulary which contains the 'missing' sound

FINDING MISSING SOUNDS: USING VOICING

For the sake of this example, our imaginary learners can produce /f/ and /v/, /s/ and /z/, /ʃ/ but not /ʒ/.

Preparation

Keep a record of words which contain the sounds learners are unable to produce. In this case we will deal with *television, measure, pleasure, garage*.

Procedure

1 Ask the class to make a long /ffffffff/ sound, then /vvvvvvvv/.
2 Ask them to repeat the sounds, this time with their fingers in their ears, so as to highlight the difference which voicing makes. Draw their attention to the fact that nothing else, apart from voicing, changes as they move from one sound to the other.
3 Ask them to make a continuous noise which changes from /f/ to /v/ and back again, and again, and so on until they run out of breath. Tell them that in doing so, they should direct their attention to maintaining the same articulation except for switching the voicing on and off.
4 Repeat the process so far with /s/ and /z/.
5 Repeat the same process with /ʃ/ and /ʒ/. They should be able to find the missing sound /ʒ/ easily.

3.7

LEVEL
Elementary +

FOCUS
Discriminating between similar sounds

MATERIALS
A worksheet (see examples opposite)

TIME
10–20 minutes

ODD ONE OUT

You can use this activity as a sounds discrimination exercise or as part of a lesson on the simple past tense, the third person of the simple present tense, or plurals.

Procedure

1 Divide the class into small groups of three or four.
2 Give each group a worksheet.
3 The learners in each group work together to agree which word in each set is different from the others and why. Note that there may be several possible answers and any valid answer is acceptable if the learners can give a reason.
4 When all the groups have finished, the whole class compares answers. The class discussion should lead to some generalisations about the sounds highlighted in the exercise. For example, voiced sounds are followed by /d/ in regular past tense endings, whilst unvoiced sounds are followed by /t/. /d/ and /t/ are themselves followed by /ɪd/ or /əd/. In the present tense, voiced sounds are followed by /z/ whilst unvoiced sounds are followed by /s/. /s/ and /z/ are themselves followed by /ɪz/, as are palatalised sounds in regular plurals.

EXTENSION

In the particular case given in Worksheet A below, use the phonemic chart (page 5) for further work on the different types of endings and their relationship with voiced and voiceless sounds, as the first two lines of consonants on the chart are clearly laid out in voiceless/voiced pair equivalents.

Worksheet A

Find the Odd One Out in the following examples. Say why it is different.

Note – the difference is in the *ending* of each word.

1 worked walked wounded watched
2 mended wanted needed gained
3 rained helped cooled robbed
4 roots looks loops moons
5 brushes mists glasses judges
6 burns hums hunts hurls
7 goes knows notes throws

Key

1 wounded (ends in /ɪd/, the others end in /t/)
2 gained (ends in /d/, the others end in /ɪd/)
3 helped (ends in /t/, the others end in /d/)
4 moons (ends in /z/, the others end in /s/)
5 mists (ends in /s/, the others end in /ɪz/)
6 hunts (ends in /s/, the others end in /z/)
7 notes (ends in /s/, the others end in /z/)

© Longman Group UK Ltd 1992

Worksheet B

Find the Odd One Out in the following examples.

Note – the difference is in the *vowel* or *diphthong* sound.

1 look foot pool cook   2 make tail pain fall
3 five give dive hive   4 work bird turn call
5 fern four port corn   6 neat need seat mate
7 here fair rare bear

Key

1 pool 2 fall 3 give 4 call 5 fern 6 mate 7 here

© Longman Group UK Ltd 1992

3.8

SOUNDS HANGMAN

You can use this activity as a warmer or a final activity. You can also use it as a vocabulary revision activity, particularly at lower levels.

LEVEL
Beginner +

FOCUS
Recognising and producing individual sounds and combinations of sounds in words

MATERIALS
A set of phoneme cards; Blu-tack or sellotape

TIME
5–20 minutes

Preparation

Select a number of cards to form a particular word, for example, /nʌmbə/. Attach the cards face down to the board with blu-tack or sellotape.

Procedure

1 Ask the learners to try and guess the sounds on the cards and produce the hidden word. They will normally attempt the most common (or familiar) sounds first, for example, /s/ or /e/.
2 If a correct sound is put forward, turn over the card in question and reattach it to the board with the phonemic symbol now visible to the class. If a sound is pronounced incorrectly, indicate this by shaking your head and saying quietly but audibly 'pronunciation'. If the sound is almost correct, indicate this by an appropriate gesture and invite the learner to try again.
3 If an incorrect suggestion is made, i.e. a correctly pronounced sound but not one on the hidden cards, you can use the same procedure as with the game 'Hangman'. With more mature learners, however, it might be advisable to introduce either a time limit (five minutes per word) or a fixed number of attempted guesses per word (ten, for example).

EXTENSION
Once the rules of the activity have been established, the learners can assume responsibility for making the hidden words themselves, with each group taking it in turns to be at the board challenging the other groups to guess their word.

VARIATION
The game can also be a team activity with each team taking it in turns to guess a sound and with points awarded to the first team to guess the hidden word correctly. It should be emphasised that phonemic symbols and not letters are used in this game.

GUESS THE PHONEME

You can use this as a simple game or warmer, or as a relatively painless way of reinforcing the pronunciation of the different phonemes.

Procedure

1 Ask the learners to stand up.
2 With blu-tack or a safety-pin, attach a phoneme card to each learner's back.
3 Ask everyone to circulate and attempt to guess the phoneme on their back by asking other learners like this: 'Is it /iː/?'. They are not allowed, of course, to say 'What phoneme have I got on my back?'.
4 The activity finishes when all the learners have guessed their own phonemes.

INITIAL 'A'

You can use this activity at most levels by varying the complexity of the vocabulary involved, but it may be particularly appropriate at lower levels where it can help to prevent consistent mispronunciation of initial 'a'. You can use it as an activity in its own right or as a quick warmer.

Procedure

1 Write up on the board a short list of example words (e.g. *apple, army, able, about, air, all, any*) which exemplify seven different pronunciations of the letter 'a' in initial position.
2 Divide the class into small groups or pairs and ask the learners to decide how each word is pronounced. You can tell them at this stage that each 'a' is pronounced differently.
3 Listen to their suggestions. Correct pronunciation if necessary. Establish that the seven sounds are: /æ/, /ɑː/, /eɪ/, /ə/, /eə/, /ɔː/ and /e/.
4 Give the class a longer list of words beginning with 'a' and ask them (again in small groups or pairs) to decide which category each of the words belongs to. This can either be done by dividing the board into columns headed by the different sounds and inviting learners to come up and add words to the appropriate columns, or by giving each group a sheet of paper with the seven columns on. One possible advantage of the latter approach is that the results can then be displayed as a permanent record and added to whenever new vocabulary with initial 'a' is encountered.

A certain amount of trial and error is an integral part of this activity! You can also encourage the learners to look for particular patterns in the pronunciation of initial 'a'. For example, the tendency of 'ar-' before a consonant or consonant cluster to be pronounced /ɑː/, and the tendency of unstressed initial 'a' to be pronounced /ə/.

3.9

LEVEL
Beginner +

FOCUS
Producing individual sounds

MATERIALS
A set of phoneme cards; Blu-tack

TIME
5 minutes

3.10

LEVEL
Beginner +

FOCUS
Different ways of pronouncing 'a' in initial position

MATERIALS
A list of words exemplifying different pronunciations of initial 'a'

TIME

EXTENSION
You can work in the same way on other letters in initial position.

3.11

LEVEL
Beginner +

FOCUS
Recognising
minimal
differences
between
individual
phonemes

MATERIALS
A minimal pairs
worksheet (see
Example tasks
below)

TIME
10–20 minutes

SOUNDS DISCRIMINATION EXERCISE

This activity can help to sensitise learners to minimal differences between individual phonemes and enable them to recognise sounds in context. It can be regarded as an initial stage in the process of learning to produce these sounds accurately. You can use it as a warmer or as a remedial slot dealing with a particular problem. It is also useful as a basic listening exercise in terms of aural training.

Procedure

1 Give each learner a copy of the worksheet and ensure that they understand you are going to read contrasting sounds or words aloud to the class and that they must decide which sound is being uttered each time and indicate this by ticking the appropriate column next to the number.
2 Read the sounds or words aloud, pausing for a short time between each one to give the learners time to make a decision.
3 Check what the learners have ticked. Repeat, if necessary, any items that are causing problems.

EXTENSION
An activation stage can follow. Depending on the level of the class, further examples can be done in small pairs or groups, with the learners taking it in turns to play the role of the teacher. That is, one learner reads out a list of sounds or words and the others tick the sounds that they hear. A valuable side-product of this stage may be that the learners will tick a sound that the speaker did not intend them to tick and will do this because of inaccurate pronunciation by the speaker. This often has the effect of focusing attention on the pronunciation of a particular sound.

Example tasks

Tick the sound you hear	Teacher reads
1 /iː/ /ɪ/	/iː/
2 /uː/ /ʊ/	/ʊ/
3 /ɜː/ /ə/	/ə/
4 /e/ /ʌ/	/ʌ/
5 /ʌ/ /æ/	/æ/
6 /ɒ/ /ɔː/	/ɒ/
7 /θ/ /ð/	/θ/
8 /eɪ/ /aɪ/	/eɪ/
9 /b/ /p/	/p/
10 /r/ /l/	/l/

© Longman Group UK Ltd 1992

Tick the word you hear			Teacher reads
1 work	walk	woke	walk
2 main	mine	moan	main
3 herd	hard	hurt	hurt
4 pole	Paul	pale	pole
5 fair	four	fear	fear

© Longman Group UK Ltd 1992

SOUNDS VOCABULARY GAME

3.12

You can use this activity as a warmer or as a final activity in which recently taught vocabulary can be practised or recycled. It also helps to focus learners on the active production of words they may recognise but not yet be able to pronounce accurately.

Preparation

You will simply need to decide on a number of general vocabulary categories (e.g. transport, nationalities, food). Note – it is advisable to try this yourself first, just to ensure that there are words containing each sound in each category.

Procedure

1 Write at least six general vocabulary categories on the board. (See example below.)
2 Divide the learners into teams of three or four as appropriate.
3 Tell them that you are going to give them a sound and that they have to find a word containing this sound for each of the six categories. The first team to do so successfully will gain one point.
4 Give them the first sound (e.g. /iː/).
5 Check that the answers given by the first team to provide a complete set of answers are correct. If they are, write up their words on the board and award them a point. If any of the set of six answers is incorrect, indicate that there is an incorrect word, but do not specify which one at this stage. Another team may now suggest their answers and will score one point if their set is correct. At this point, deal with any errors in the previous suggestions.
6 Continue with further sounds. The team with the most points at the end is the winner.

The board might look something like this after two rounds using the sounds /iː/ and /e/, for example:

	Food	Language	Part of Body	Sport	Animal	Colour
/iː/:	cheese	Greek	cheek	skiing	sheep	green
/e/:	bread	French	leg	tennis	hen	red

LEVEL
Elementary +

FOCUS
Pronouncing known vocabulary

MATERIALS
None

TIME
10–20 minutes

3.13

LEVEL
Elementary +

FOCUS
Recognising sounds;
Combining sounds into words

MATERIALS
A list of words transcribed into phonemic script and then jumbled into anagrams (see examples below)

TIME
10–20 minutes

SOUNDS ANAGRAM RACE

You can use this exercise for a number of purposes. It can function as a game or a warmer (a time limit may help in this respect). You can use it as a means of recycling previously taught vocabulary. You can also use it as a relatively painless way of focusing on combinations of sounds that may be problematic for a particular learner or group of learners (for example, consonant clusters in initial position).

Preparation

Nothing beyond making lists of anagrams.

Procedure

1 Divide the learners into pairs or small groups.
2 Give each pair or group a copy of the list of anagrams (alternatively, to save paper, write it on the board or show it on an OHP).
3 Ask the learners to reorder the sounds in the sound anagrams to produce words. A certain amount of discussion and experimentation will be necessary, and there may also be several possibilities. Ask the learners to note down the phonemes in the correct order first and then to write the corresponding word next to it in normal script.
4 When all the pairs or groups have completed the exercise, ask the learners to come out and write their suggested answers on the board. The class as a whole can then discuss whether the answers are correct.

Examples (all verbs)

etəssdʒ   aʊlə
mɑsrpɪ   mmrɪəbe
dnetɪn   ʌɪsskd
lkəneɪpm   əuːsjdɪrtn
skrwetɪ   ktprɪdə

Key:
suggest   allow
promise   remember
intend   discuss
complain   introduce
request   predict

© Longman Group UK Ltd 1992

SOUNDS BINGO

Preparation

Preparation time can be reduced if you give all the learners the same Sounds Bingo worksheet and ask them to delete at random five sounds before the activity starts. This obviates the need to produce a different card for each learner.

Procedure

1 Give each learner a copy of the Sounds Bingo worksheet (see example below).
2 Tell the learners that you will randomly pronounce sounds from the phonemic chart (e.g. Number 1 – /e/; Number 2 – /m/). If they hear a sound which is on their card, they should write the corresponding number next to the sound. Keep a numbered list of the sounds you pronounce in the order you pronounce them. This helps with checking the learners' work.
3 The winner is the first one to number correctly all the sounds on their card.
4 Check that the winner has crossed out the correct sounds. If not, the game continues.

3.14

LEVEL
Beginner +

FOCUS
Recognising sounds

MATERIALS
One Sounds Bingo worksheet per learner

TIME
15–30 minutes

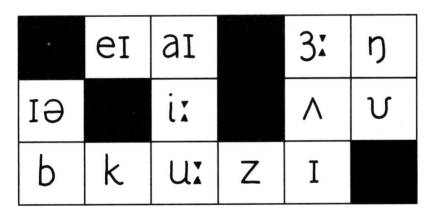

Fig. 5 Example of a Sounds Bingo card

VARIATIONS

1 The same procedure can be applied with minimal pairs/minimal groups replacing the single sounds on the bingo cards, for example:

work	walk	week	woke
put	port	pert	putt
hat	heart	hard	had
fill	feel	full	fool
pall	pole	pull	pool

© Longman Group UK Ltd 1992

Again, ask the learners to delete at random five of the words before starting the game. This should ensure that all the cards are different.

2 Sounds Bingo can also be played in small groups with one learner reading out the list of sounds or words to the rest of the group. This brings a production element to the exercise and also a degree of peer monitoring of pronunciation. There is likely to be considerable healthy discussion about the pronunciation of various sounds!

CHAPTER 4

Spelling to sound and back again

SOUNDS MAZE

Preparation

Ten minutes to prepare the maze.

Procedure

1 Divide the class into pairs.
2 Give each pair a maze worksheet. (See Fig. 6 below.)

f	r	e	n	d	l	ɪ	n	ə	s	æ	t
l	ʊ	n	ʌ	r	uː	m	j	e	s	ɪ	k
e	m	t	ɪ	ɪ	p	æ	uː	r	l	p	æ
k	e	ə	b	l	iː	d	z	ɪ	p	iː	r
s	t	ɒ	p	ɔː	ɔɪ	ɪ	r	p	m	e	t
ɪ	s	p	ɪ	l	l	t	aɪ	m	t	iː	n
b	ɪ	l	d	ɪ	ŋ	r	eɪ	ʌ	l	d	ɒ
ɪ	iː	r	t	ɔː	k	k	æ	b	l	æ	k
l	aɪ	t	b	ʌ	l	b	eɪ	p	n	ɜː	t
ɪ	l	n	t	eɪ	ʌ	l	iː	t	s	k	əʊ
t	r	eɪ	n	t	r	ʌ	k	ɪ	aɪ	iː	m
ɪ	m	p	ɒ	s	ɪ	b	ɪ	l	ɪ	t	ɪ

Fig. 6 Example of a Sounds Maze worksheet

© Longman Group UK Ltd 1992

4.1

LEVEL
Beginner +

FOCUS
Recognising phonemic symbols; Relationships between sounds and spelling

MATERIALS
One Sounds Maze worksheet per pair of learners

TIME
20–30 minutes

3 Tell the class that the phonemic maze contains, for example, the names of ten countries. These are hidden in the maze and may be horizontal, vertical or diagonal. They may also be from left to right or right to left, and from top to bottom or bottom to top.

4 The first pair to discover all ten words are the winners.

4.2

LEVEL
Beginner +

FOCUS
Relationships
between sounds
and spelling;
Practice in the
pronunciation of
sounds in words

MATERIALS
One set of
phoneme cards
and one set of
word cards per
group of 4
learners

TIME
15–20 minutes

PHONEMIC SNAP

Preparation

Fifteen minutes to prepare the word cards.

Procedure

1 Divide the learners into groups of four, preferably with each group around a table. All the groups work simultaneously.

2 Give each group a set of phoneme cards and a set of word cards. The word cards could contain recently presented vocabulary and could thus be a means of reinforcing/practising it. The cards could, on the other hand, also contain new items of vocabulary, thus introducing a more cognitive element to the game, in which learners are required to make appropriate guesses about the pronunciation of new vocabulary items.

3 Ask each group to place both sets of cards face down on the table, with the phoneme cards on the left. In turn, the learners turn over first one phoneme card and then one word card. They continue to do this until the phoneme on the upturned phoneme card matches one of the sounds contained in the word on the word card. At this point, any one of the four may shout 'Snap'. If the group agrees that the call is correct, then the learner who called 'Snap' keeps the two cards in question. In the event of disagreement they should consult you!

4 When the bottom of each pack has been reached, the cards are shuffled and the game continues.

5 At the end of the game, the learner with the most cards is the winner.

RHYMING SOUNDS

Preparation

Write an example of a word-ending (including a vowel) in bold phonemic script at the top of each sheet of A3 paper.

Procedure

1 Take one sheet of A3 paper as an example and invite the learners to think of a word or words ending in the phoneme or phonemes shown at the top of the sheet.
2 Elicit correct examples from the learners in ordinary spelling on each sheet. (See examples below.)
3 Divide the learners into groups of three or four.
4 Give each group a sheet.
5 They add as many words to the rhyming lists as they can, checking in the dictionary or with you as required.
6 When each group has exhausted a particular sound, they pass the sheet on to the next group and this group adds any new words they have before passing it on to the next group and so on.
7 Display the sheets prominently in the classroom. Learners can then add to them whenever an appropriate new item of vocabulary comes up. The visual element of the display is intended to reinforce the patterns in question and the sound/spelling relationships which they exemplify.

Examples

/-aɪt/	/-ɔːt/	/-eɪn/	/-ɔː/
night	taught	reign	bore
light	bought	rain	boar
white	fort	lane	law
site	taut	entertain	roar
bright	sort	explain	core
polite	nought	plane	four

4.3

LEVEL
Elementary +

FOCUS
Links between sounds and spelling; Recognising sound/spelling patterns

MATERIALS
Several sheets of A3 paper; Blu-tack or similar

TIME
Ongoing over a whole course

4.4

LEVEL
Any

FOCUS
Relationships
between
pronunciation and
spelling

MATERIALS
Marker pens of as
many different
colours as
possible; Large
sheets of paper
(flipchart paper is
ideal); Some wall
space to stick
them on

TIME
Ongoing
throughout a
course

ONGOING VOCABULARY RECORD

Procedure

1 Use the sheets of paper to make an ongoing record of words introduced or practised during a course. You can do this during class time or as part of your own preparation. Just write the words one after another, big enough to be seen clearly from all parts of the classroom. Use normal spelling, but colour code the vowels, so that identical vowel sounds appear in the same colour regardless of how they are spelt. For example, the 'a' of *want*, the 'ou' of *cough* and the 'o' of *lot* will all be the same colour. Similarly, the 'a' of *along*, the 'ur' of *Saturday* and the 'er' of *butter* will share the same colour.

2 You can indicate stressed syllables by underlining, italicising, etc.

EXTENSION
Once the system is initiated, it can be taken over by the learners, who can use dictionaries to check pronunciations. The charts can be used both overtly, for particular exercises, and/or as wallpaper whose patterns and colours subconsciously imprint themselves.

VARIATION
Limit the use of colour coding to certain vowels only, or apply it to some consonant sounds too. All the letters of a word which are not colour coded can be written in black.

ACKNOWLEDGEMENT
This idea was suggested by the Silent Way word charts and by the use of peripheral visuals in Suggestopedia.

SOUNDS SEARCH

You can use Sounds Search as a warmer or as a final activity. Like *Sounds Hangman* (3.8), it can also be used for vocabulary revision.

Procedure

1 Divide the class into groups of three or four.
2 Give each group a set of phoneme cards and ask them to spread the cards out on the table or on the floor.
3 Read out a list of words.
4 As each word is read out, each group attempts to 'spell' it as quickly as possible with the phoneme cards.
5 The first group to make the word correctly gets a point.
6 The complexity of the vocabulary can clearly be varied and you should make sure that there are sufficient phoneme cards in each set to cover the words you read out. For example, if a word contains two /t/ sounds, then there should be at least two /t/ cards in the set.

VARIATION
In small classes the same activity can be done on an individual basis.

4.5

LEVEL
Beginner +

FOCUS
Recognising individual sounds and relating sounds to spelling

MATERIALS
Set of phoneme cards per group of learners;
List of words

TIME
5–15 minutes

4.6

LEVEL
Elementary +

FOCUS
Relationships
between sounds
and spelling

MATERIALS
A set of phoneme
cards and a table
per group of 4
learners

TIME
15–45 minutes

SOUNDS SCRABBLE

This activity gives learners practice in combining sounds to form recognisable utterances. It can also increase their awareness of frequent phenomena, such as the representation of final '-er' in spelling by the phoneme /ə/. You can use Sounds Scrabble as a warmer (given prior familiarity with the phonemic symbols), as a quick revision activity (for new lexis), as a stage in a lesson dealing with sounds and spelling, or as a language game at any appropriate stage in a longer lesson.

Procedure

1 Divide the learners into groups of four, preferably round small tables.
2 Appoint a scorer for each group.
3 Give each group a set of phoneme cards.
4 They place the set of cards face down on the table. Each learner in turn selects six cards from the pack, leaving twenty cards in the pack. Tell everyone to ensure that other members of the group cannot see their cards.
5 Player 1 in each group then attempts to make a word of two syllables or more on the table. If this player is unable to make a word of any sort with the cards they have, then they discard one card by placing it at the bottom of the pack and taking one new card from the top of the pack. The game then passes to Player 2 in each group. If, however, Player 1 can make a word, then one point is scored for each card used. Player 1 then takes the same number of cards from the top of the pack that they have used to make their word and the game passes to Player 2 in each group.
6 The other players then take it in turn to extend the word or build on it crosswise, by including at least one sound used in the first word, and so on in subsequent turns. (See Fig. 7 opposite for an example of what a grid might look like.)
7 When all the cards in the pack have been used, the winner is the player with the highest points total.
8 Your role is to monitor the groups, ensure that the words are correct and help any learners who may need assistance.

EXTENSION
Learners transcribe some of the longer or more interesting words into correct English spelling. This can be made more interesting if groups transcribe the words from another group's grid. This follow-up activity gives further practice in sensitising learners to the relationships between sounds and spelling in English.

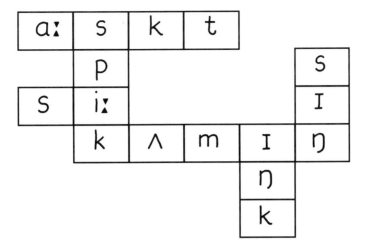

Fig. 7 Example of a Sounds Scrabble grid

USING SOUNDS FOR WORD BUILDING

You can use this activity both to practise the sounds of known words and to encourage learners to experiment and generate new words. It is particularly fruitful in the area of homophones (e.g. *blue/blew*). The exercise is a cognitive, student-centred activity and you may find that it takes quite a lot of time. Your own role is as instigator and monitor, giving help where needed.

Procedure

1 Divide the learners into pairs or small groups.
2 Give each group the same collection of two or three 'sound frames'. For example:
/m—t/ /p—t/ /p—n/ /s—t/ /b—d/ /f—l/ /k—t/
The dash represents a missing vowel or diphthong sound.
3 Tell the learners to experiment by trying out different vowel or consonant sounds in the 'sound frames' you have given them. At first, they will probably come up with a few familiar words. In the case of /m—t/, for example, these might be /miːt/ and /met/.
4 Ask them to note down both the phonemic spelling of the words they think are possible and then the normal spelling of each word. After they have exhausted known words, they should produce some further tentative examples. In the case of /m—t/, they may possibly produce /meɪt/, /muːt/ and /mæt/. Here the normal spelling may be more problematic and they may need recourse to a dictionary to check the various possibilities. You may find they will also ask you questions, such as 'Is there such a word as *moot*?'

4.7

LEVEL
Elementary +

FOCUS
Relationships
between sounds
and spelling

MATERIALS
A list of 'sound
frames' (see
examples below);
A number of
monolingual
dictionaries

TIME
20–45 minutes

5 Ask the groups to note down the meaning of any new words.
6 The groups pool their answers on the board. At this point, any spelling mistakes can be corrected (by other learners preferably but by you if necessary) and any problems with meaning can also be dealt with.

VARIATIONS
1 The activity can also be turned into a word game, particularly at higher levels, by awarding points for each correct suggestion. The group with the most correct words wins the game.
2 Give different 'sound frames' to different groups, thus extending the eventual word pool on the board.

4.8

LEVEL
Elementary +

FOCUS
Relationships between sounds and spelling

MATERIALS
An empty crossword grid;
A set of clues (See Fig. 8a)

TIME
30–45 minutes

SOUNDS CROSSWORDS

This activity can form the major part of a lesson devoted to practising sounds. It can also be used as a means of practising or revising items of vocabulary, particularly as regards their pronunciation.

Procedure

1 Divide the class into pairs or small groups.
2 Give each group a copy of the crossword grid and a set of clues.
3 The learners then work on the task using dictionaries (preferably monolingual) as required. Ensure that they know they are supposed to fill the grid in using phonemic symbols and not letters. They will normally arrive at the word in question first and then discuss, perhaps experimenting with the pronunciation, exactly how it is pronounced and what symbol is required.
4 Monitor progress as necessary.
5 The groups compare their answers.

VARIATION
An additional 'information gap' element can be introduced by providing each group or pair with some of the clues only. They then need to interact with other groups in order to complete the puzzle.

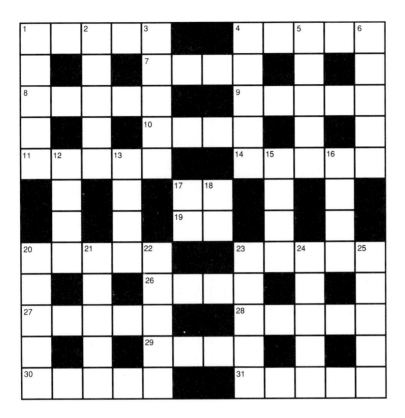

Clues:

ACROSS

1 Capital of France
4 Name and —
7 It is the editor's job to — a newspaper
8 Yellow fruit
9 Ordinary
10 A rough path
11 The person who sends a letter or parcel
14 To make tighter
17 Past tense of see
19 Past tense of eat
20 Past tense of film
23 Electrical wire
26 Dreadful
27 Way out
28 Britain is an —
29 Avoid
30 Illness
31 3rd person singular of swim

DOWN

1 You should report a robbery to the —
2 An inhabitant of Rome
3 Middle
4 Opposite of defended
5 Write again
6 A short stay
12 Each
13 A nightmare is a bad —
15 Part of the eye
16 Infinitive of 4 down
17 Speak
18 Similar to should as in 'I — to go'
20 Opposite of enemy
21 Opposite of wins
22 Sons and —
23 All — from Heathrow are subject to delay
24 Electricity is a form of —
25 Inhabitants of Saudi Arabia

Fig. 8a Example of a Sounds Crossword

© Longman Group UK Ltd 1992

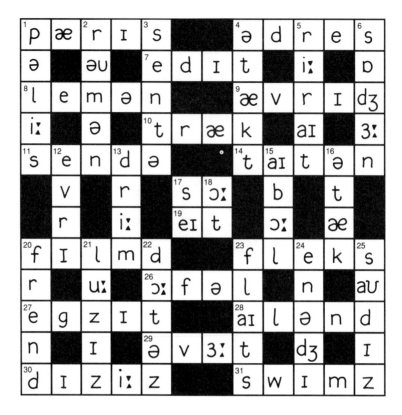

Fig. 8b Example of a Sounds Crossword (Key)

© Longman Group UK Ltd 1992

4.9 PHONEMIC WORD RACE

LEVEL
Beginner +

FOCUS
Relationships
between sounds
and spelling

MATERIALS
None

TIME
15–30 minutes

You can use this activity to sensitise learners to the relationships between sounds and spelling, particularly the different ways in which a specific sound may be represented in written form. It is also a useful means of recycling and revising previously learnt vocabulary.

Procedure

1 Divide the learners into pairs or groups of three.
2 Set a time limit, ideally fairly short, such as 5 minutes, as the activity is intended to be a race.
3 Ask each pair or group to elect a 'scribe'.
4 Ask the learners to think of as many words as they can containing a particular sound (e.g. /æ/) in the time available. The scribes should write down the words for their groups.
5 When the time is up, the pair or group with the largest number of correct words is awarded a point.
6 Continue with other sounds.

CHAPTER 5

Sounds in sequence

ASSIMILATION AWARENESS EXERCISE

This exercise is intended to sensitise learners to changes to and disappearances of sounds as a result of their environment. It can be part of a lesson focusing on oral fluency and natural rhythm through linking words together. Learners are often unaware, for example, that the final /t/ of 'first' in *first light* disappears in rapid speech. You may find it helpful to contrast the different sounds of *first light* with the /t/ of 'first' pronounced clearly and then with the same sound disappearing.

Procedure

1 Give each learner a copy of this worksheet containing the following (example) questions:

In rapid speech:
1 When is a /n/ a /m/?
2 When is a /t/ a /p/?
3 When is a /d/ a /b/?
4 When is a /s/ a /ʃ/?
5 When is a /z/ a /ʒ/?
6 When is a /n/ a /ŋ/?
7 When is a /d/ a /g/?
8 When is a /t/ a /k/?
© Longman Group UK Ltd 1992

2 Give each learner a jumbled list of examples where such assimilations take place.

Examples

ten green bottles	she was born in
ten pin bowling	Birmingham
she has, has she?	the right key
this shirt	white paper
good boy	ten players
good girl	bit part
good morning	speed boat

© Longman Group UK Ltd 1992

5.1

LEVEL
Elementary +

FOCUS
Awareness of features of connected speech

MATERIALS
A worksheet with tasks and examples (see below)

TIME
10–20 minutes

3 Read aloud the list of examples. You can either read the examples in the order given in the worksheet above (for recognition purposes only), or in a jumbled order for a more demanding listening activity.

4 Ask the learners to work in pairs. Give each pair a jumbled list of further examples where the above assimilations occur. One learner reads the examples aloud and together they match the examples with the numbers above.

Further examples

hot pie	this shop
bad manners	good goal
in Bolton	hot grog
does she?	ten girls

© Longman Group UK Ltd 1992

5 Class discussion. You may need to give further examples. You may also need to explain why this happens! One explanation is that the speech organs get into position for the following sound and thus the first sound may take on some of the characteristics of the following sound. For example, in *good morning*, the lips may be closed during 'good' in anticipation of the following /m/, causing the /d/ sound to resemble /b/.

6 Ask the learners to listen to what happens to the final /t/ sound of the first word in the following examples.

first time	last chance	first light
next week	best team	ghost train
dust sheet	worst type	just one

© Longman Group UK Ltd 1992

7 Production. Ask learners to practise saying the examples. Emphasise the element of speed – the final /t/ disappears in *rapid* speech.

5.2

LEVEL
Elementary +

FOCUS
Producing weak forms

MATERIALS
None

TIME
10–20 minutes

PRODUCING WEAK FORMS

One problem for foreign learners of English is that they often tend to give full value to unstressed syllables, particularly those which contain the unstressed /ə/ sound. You can use this exercise to heighten their awareness of the frequency of unstressed syllables and also to improve the rhythm of their speech in short utterances containing unstressed and elided sounds.

Preparation

You will need a list of phrases, expressions and short sentences containing unstressed syllables (see examples opposite). Write up your examples in *phonemic script* on the board (10–12 examples should be sufficient).

Examples:

əpiːsəkeɪk   lɒrəlnhaːdɪ

fɪʃntʃɪps   rednwaɪt

tentəwʌn   faɪvtənaɪn

əpækɪtəkrɪsps   hɪzfrəmlʌndn

əbɒtləbɪə   ələufəbred

brednbʌtə   twentɪtətuː

Procedure

1 Ask the learners to try saying the above expressions to each other in pairs or small groups. This is to give them the opportunity to work out how to say them and to experiment with producing the sounds in the relative security of a small group rather than before the whole class.

2 Go round the groups and monitor progress.

3 Invite suggestions from the class as a whole. If any suggestions contain a sound which is not in the transcription (e.g. pronouncing the /d/ in *and*), you can question this. 'Why are you saying *and*? There isn't a /d/ sound, is there?'

EXTENSION

For further practice of the production of weak, unstressed forms, you can play a simple game. Start by saying 'I went to the supermarket and bought a bottle of wine'. The sentence now goes round the whole class with each learner repeating your first sentence and then adding a new phrase of their own. Thus the second learner might say, 'I went to the supermarket and bought a bottle of wine and a packet of crisps'. The third learner might go on, 'I went to the supermarket and bought a bottle of wine, a packet of crisps and a loaf of bread', and so on until every learner has contributed. /ɒv/ is not allowed! /əv/ is tolerated, but /ə/ is preferred! (Of course, /əv/ is correct before a vowel sound.)

5.3

LEVEL
Beginner +

FOCUS
Stressed syllables
and weak forms

MATERIALS
Tape recorder;
Blank tape (more
than one recorder
and several tapes
for the Extension
option);
Transcript of
recording;
Language
laboratory for
Extension option

TIME
30–60 minutes

USING LISTENING MATERIAL

Preparation

You will need to record a short piece of off-air listening material (2–3 minutes maximum) and to prepare a transcript of the text. You can use short recordings of authentic listening material (for example, the news headlines from the radio) to heighten learners' awareness of stress placement and the widespread occurrence of unstressed syllables (especially /ə/) in English.

Procedure

1 Give the learners a copy of the tapescript. Divide them into pairs and ask them to mark where they think the main stresses will fall.

2 Go through the learners' suggestions with the whole group. Some discussion of why they think the stresses will fall in the places they suggest will normally be profitable (important words, the last word in the sentence, the main verb as opposed to an auxiliary, a contrastive stress, and so on).

3 Tell them that they are now going to listen to the tape. Ask them to compare the stress placement on the tape with the stress placement they have predicted.

4 Play the tape. You will probably need to play it more than once, and possibly several times.

5 Ask the learners to compare their answers in pairs or small groups.

6 Check that all the learners have the correct answers. Play the tape again if there are any problems.

7 Now ask the learners to listen to the tape again and to underline all the weak /ə/ sounds that occur between the stressed syllables.

8 Play the tape (more than once if necessary). Get the learners to compare their answers and check that their suggestions are correct. There will normally be a large number of unstressed /ə/ sounds.

9 Ask the learners to group the unstressed words according to their function. This should produce categories such as prepositions (e.g. *to, from, of, at,* and *for*), conjunctions (*and, but, that*), auxiliary verbs (*be, do, have*) and some modal auxiliaries (*should, could, would, must*). At this stage it is also worth discussing when such words *are* stressed (e.g. for emphasis or contrast).

EXTENSION

The learners can each be asked to record the text onto a blank tape and then to compare their version with the original. You can also ask them to 'shadow read' the text, i.e. read it aloud as the text is being played on the tape recorder (see 7.8 *Shadowing*). If you have access to a language laboratory, this is an ideal venue for these activities, as learners can work at their own pace and repeat their own recording as often as they feel necessary. You can also record the text onto the laboratory master tape in short sections, which the learners can then repeat immediately afterwards. Throughout this activity, the particular focus is on stress placement and weak forms, but other aspects of pronunciation are also being worked on.

HOW MANY WORDS?

LEVEL
Elementary +

When confronted with conversational English spoken at normal speed, many learners find it extremely difficult to interpret utterances which are well within their competence as regards the grammar and vocabulary they have learnt.

FOCUS
Interpreting sounds in fast colloquial speech

Examples
What d'you want?
I wouldn't have done that.
How much longer're you gonna be?
Have you seen her yet?

MATERIALS
A list of sentences which are not difficult for your class in terms of grammar or vocabulary, but which contain features of pronunciation, when they are pronounced naturally, which are likely to confuse listening. For example, weak forms, elision, assimilation, linking.

The problem is exacerbated by teaching which only presents sloweddown, over-articulated models where every word and sound is clearly identifiable. Here we suggest a way of devoting a few minutes from time to time to some intensive work on this problem.

Procedure

1 Dictate the sentence quickly, casually, colloquially, even unclearly, as it might occur in the middle of a conversation.
2 Learners write it down, or as much as they can, and if necessary, try to reconstruct the rest through discussion with their neighbours. If they cannot identify a particular word, assure them that they do in fact know the word, and encourage them not only to work on what their ears heard, but also on their knowledge of what the word could be.
3 If necessary, dictate the sentence again, being careful not to overarticulate or slow down in order to 'help'.
4 Ask the class how many words there were in the sentence. If there is disagreement, this is likely to provoke further discussion. If there is a fair measure of agreement, invite volunteers to write their versions of the sentence on the board.
5 Ask the class to adjudicate on which of the offered versions are grammatically possible.
6 Read out each of the possible versions, and then your original sentence for comparison. Ask the class which version was yours.

TIME
10–15 minutes

RATIONALE
Learners sometimes panic and become unable to understand anything at all. This activity encourages them to work on their understanding of a short burst of English, with time for reflection and rehearing, piecing

together an interpretation based on their knowledge of what is grammatically or semantically possible (or likely), plus the imperfect sound clues they actually hear.

5.5

LEVEL
Elementary +

FOCUS
Sensitising learners to assimilation and elision; Changes in the pronunciation of some words in connected speech

MATERIALS
See *Preparation*

TIME
10–20 minutes

CONNECTED SPEECH DICTATION

Learners of English, even advanced ones, are often not aware of all the processes of simplification in connected speech, including elision, assimilation, vowel reduction and the creation of weak forms. This activity should be carried out in a light-hearted manner!

Preparation

You need a list of phrases which illustrate simplifications in connected speech. Choose your own, if possible including examples which you have noticed learners pronouncing in an exaggerated, hypercorrect way. Here is a sample list:

goodbye	/d/ becomes /b/
good grief	/d/ becomes /g/
Do you have to go?	'have' becomes /hæf/
rock and roll	'and' becomes /n/
Do you want some?	'do you' becomes /djə/ or /dʒə/
Can you help me?	'can' becomes /kən/ or /kn/
a pint of bitter	'of' becomes /əv/ or /ə/
Is he there?	'he' becomes /ɪ/
Shall we go?	'Shall we' becomes /ʃwɪ/

Procedure

1 Tell the class you are going to dictate some words to them. Ask them to prepare by putting numbers from one to nine (or however many items you are going to dictate) down the left-hand side of the page.
2 For each item, dictate only the word illustrating the connected speech feature, twice, to give them a good chance to hear. Tell them these are normal English words, and they should use normal spelling. From our sample list above, you dictate only:

/gʊb/
/gʊg/
/hæf/
/n/
/djə/
/kən/
/əv/
/ɪ/
/ʃwɪ/

3 Ask the class to compare with each other what they have written.

4 Now tell them you are going to dictate short phrases and sentences, each of which contains one of the items dictated earlier. They should write these down the right-hand side of the paper so that each phrase or sentence is on the same line as the item it contains.

5 Now dictate the complete phrases/sentences, making sure the pronunciation of the originally-dictated word stays the same as before.

6 Again, get learners to compare answers with each other.

7 Ask them to comment on what they have heard and what they have written.

EXTENSION

If the learners seem keen, they can try to imitate the pronunciation of the phrases/sentences.

RATIONALE

Of course it is unusual to give these words their connected speech forms when they are spoken in isolation. But the point is that this is a way of forcing learners' awareness of this aspect of English pronunciation. It is important for both teachers and learners to bear in mind, however, that the kinds of pronunciations exemplified in the exercise are not obligatory, either for native speakers or for foreign learners. For the learners, the most important thing is that an awareness of these features will help them to be able to interpret informal spoken English. Whether or not they want to emulate these features in their own speech is a matter of personal preference.

COMPLETING LIMERICKS

5.6

LEVEL
Beginner +

FOCUS
Rhythm, syllable reduction and rhyme

MATERIALS
A limerick – traditional or homemade

TIME
Variable

The regular rhythm of a limerick is obviously not the same as the normal rhythms of spontaneous speech. But using limericks can help to give learners an awareness of the kinds of rhythmic patterns which they need to put into practice in a more dynamic way when they speak English. In particular, the exercises that follow can help to show how unstressed syllables are compressed into the spaces between the stresses.

Procedure

1 Show a limerick, with one line missing, on the board or OHP or on a handout given to groups of learners. For example:

There was a young fellow called Bright
Who could travel faster than light
He set off one day
In a relative way

....

© Longman Group UK Ltd 1992

2 Ask them to propose suitable lines to complete the limerick, and to judge the suitability of each others' suggestions (paying attention to meaning as well as pronunciation). It will be clear which versions have the correct rhyme scheme and can be said with the correct rhythm.

3 The class can then practise reciting accepted versions, tapping or beating the rhythm as they do so.

VARIATIONS

1 The missing line need not be the last; it could be any of the lines.

2 Instead of one line, leave out two, or three, or four.

3 Instead of a line, leave out words or phrases.

4 Give a complete limerick, but with a line or phrase which does not fit, and which the learners must identify and replace.

5 Specify the number of words to be supplied. For example: – – – – –

6 Specify the number of syllables to be supplied. For example:
 * ** * *** *

7 Specify the number of syllables and their relationship with the rhythm. For example: o oO o ooo O

8 Ask each group of learners to write limericks and swap incomplete versions with other groups. They then complete the incomplete limericks.

9 Challenge them to supply a line containing as many syllables as possible, while still conforming to the rhythm. A metronome can be used to check this.

CHAPTER 6

Word stress

INTRODUCING WORD STRESS

An appreciation of what stress is is an important prerequisite for learning to pronounce words correctly. Here the concept is introduced through a non-intellectual, guided discovery approach.

Procedure

Invite the learners to propose words with two syllables and represent these words by putting rods on the table, sorted into two groups according to stress patterns. For example, *never, always, wanted* and *English* would go together, and *along, because, collect* and *predict* would go together. If this activity follows on from *Introducing syllables* (2.8), you can use the two-syllable words already on the table. Ask the learners to recall them one by one and to sort them into two groups as appropriate. If the sample of words is sufficiently large, it should be visibly apparent that the majority of two-syllable words are stressed on the first syllable.

EXTENSION
Use the example words to teach language such as:

Which syllable is stressed?
The stress is on the *n*th syllable.
The *n*th syllable is stressed.

This can then become part of your standard classroom metalanguage.

VARIATION
Use three-syllable words. In this case it should be apparent that very few words are stressed on the third syllable.

6.1

LEVEL
Most obviously applicable to near-beginners, but may be needed at any level

FOCUS
Introducing the concept of stress

MATERIALS
A table; Some Cuisenaire rods or similar (see page 8)

TIME
About 15 minutes

6.2

LEVEL
Beginner +

FOCUS
Word stress
patterns in
English

MATERIALS
Several sheets of
A3 paper; Blu-tack
or similar;
Coloured pens

TIME
Ongoing over a
whole course

STRESS PATTERNS

The aim of this activity is to increase learners' awareness of the word stress patterns of English and help them to recognise and reproduce particular patterns. The examples can be referred to (and added to) whenever it seems appropriate to do so.

Procedure

1 Present five or six typical word stress patterns. A useful device is to use words which can then act as memory aids; for example, the names of countries (Scotland, Japan, Indonesia).

2 Represent each pattern visually (e.g. *El Salvador* o O o o). Write this pattern boldly, along with the name of the country, at the top of a sheet of A3 paper. Repeat the process for each of the stress patterns.

3 Invite the learners to think of a further example for each pattern. Initially these could be other geographical names that conform to the corresponding patterns, but any vocabulary items can be used equally well.

4 Divide the learners into groups of three or four and give each group one of the sheets. Each group will have a different pattern represented by a different country name (see examples below).

5 Ask the groups to add to the list in front of them. Monitor to check that their additions are correct. When they can find no more examples, they pass the sheet on to the next group who, in turn, add their examples of this particular pattern. Continue until all the groups have added something to each of the patterns. Note that all the groups should be working simultaneously!

6 Display the sheets prominently in the classroom and encourage learners to add to them whenever a new item of vocabulary comes up in class.

Examples

El ˈSalvador	ˈScotland	Iˈran	ˈSwitzerland
intelligent	fortune	prefer	fortunate
uncomfortable	classroom	divide	comfortable
impossible	hopeless	correct	vegetable
unbreakable	pattern	display	dictionary
appropriate	lesson	confirm	wonderful

WORD STRESS AWARENESS EXERCISE

The aim of this activity is to give learners practice in placing word stress correctly. It is particularly suitable for recycling vocabulary with difficult or unusual stress placement, and also for working on stress errors common to a particular group or nationality.

Procedure

1 Divide the class into pairs or small groups.
2 Give each pair or small group a list of words (on a photocopied sheet or written on the board) with the stress incorrectly marked.
3 Tell them that in every case the stress is marked on the wrong syllable and that they should work together to establish where the correct stress should fall in each case.
4 When they have completed the task, the different pairs or groups compare their answers.

VARIATIONS

1 This activity can be made more demanding by including some words with the stress correctly marked. Don't forget to tell your learners that some are right and some are wrong!
2 New vocabulary items can also be introduced into the activity.

6.3

LEVEL
Elementary +

FOCUS
Recognising and producing correct stress placement

MATERIALS
A list of multi-syllabic words

TIME
15 minutes

GUESS THE STRESS

This procedure is an adjunct to work on vocabulary which the learners find, or the teacher presents, in its written form.

Procedure

1 When the question of how to pronounce a new multi-syllabic word arises, ask the class how many syllables they think there are in it. There may be disagreement about this. If necessary, you can resolve the issue.
2 Ask which syllable they think is stressed. If they are right, they can practise pronouncing it (paying attention to the correct sounds as well, of course) and the activity is finished.
3 If not, say the word with the stress in all possible positions in turn (e.g. say *participant* as par̲ticipant, par̲ticipant, partic̲ipant and particip̲ant). The class then vote on which stress they think is most likely. (They might want to hear the possibilities again.)
4 Count the votes and announce the correct version, or let the class find it in dictionaries.

6.4

LEVEL
Any

FOCUS
Predicting word stress

MATERIALS
None

TIME
Variable

REQUIREMENT
Previous work on the nature and metalanguage of syllables and stress

EXTENSION

When learners are used to this idea, they can take on the job of producing all the possible versions.

VARIATION

You can add a visual dimension to the parade of possible pronunciations by illustrating each one on the board or OHP (*participant* = Oooo, oOoo, ooOo, oooO) or by using rods on a table.

RATIONALE

1 A group of learners, even one with very little experience of English, has an uncanny ability to be collectively right.
2 English pronunciation is not as chaotic and unpredictable as it is sometimes made out to be. There are rules and tendencies in the realm of word stress (see Kreidler, 1989 and Poldauf, 1984). It is probably helpful to draw learners' attention to some of these at some stage. But the procedure advocated here allows them to internalise these rules and tendencies by developing their own inner criteria.

6.5

LEVEL
Elementary +

FOCUS
Accurate stress placement

MATERIALS
Word cards and stress symbol cards (see *Preparation*)

TIME
10 minutes

STRESS MATCHING GAME

You can use this activity either as a warmer or as a means of reinforcing the pronunciation of recently taught vocabulary.

Preparation

Prepare two sets of cards. On one set write a single multi-syllabic word on each card. On the other set, write the stress patterns of each of these words represented with symbols. For example, *information* would appear as ooOo and *phonology* as oOoo. Two or three words per learner should be sufficient.

Procedure

1 Mix the cards in each set.
2 Give each learner two or three word cards and a corresponding number of non-matching stress symbol cards.
3 Tell the learners to find the stress symbol cards that match their word cards. They are likely to need language such as 'Could you say your word?' and 'It doesn't match.'
4 Ask the learners to stand up and find their matching cards. This is a mingling exercise and they may need to speak to several other learners before they find their cards. When they find a matching card, they retain the word card and take the stress symbol card from the other learner. The activity continues until each learner has obtained a stress symbol card for each of their word cards.

5 When all the learners have found their matching cards, check that they have the correct answers. An effective way of doing this is to get them to stick their pairs of cards on the board with blu-tack or something similar. You can then invite the whole group to give their opinions on whether the pairs are correctly matched or not.

VOCABULARY REVISION

A lot of work with vocabulary focuses on meaning. Of course this is vital, but we should not neglect other aspects of learning vocabulary. This is a vocabulary revision activity which works on accuracy of pronunciation.

Preparation

Draw up a list of vocabulary items which you want the class to revise or to recall as the basis for further work. The items could, for example, form part of a lexical set which has recently been introduced, or be associated with a story.

Procedure

1 Ask the learners to recall and write down one vocabulary item from a certain set or source for each of the following syllable/stress patterns:

O Oo oO
Ooo oOo ooO
Oooo oOoo ooOo

If the chosen source of vocabulary was, say, a recently-read story about a missing letter, examples of these patterns might be:

stamp contents reply
envelope collection redirect
fortunately delivery compensation

2 Gather the suggestions of different members of the class on the board.
3 If necessary, get the class to practise pronouncing the words.
4 Say, or write on the board, any other relevant vocabulary which you think is important but which the learners have not suggested. Ask them to allocate it to the correct categories.
5 Move on to any further activity you have in mind using the collected vocabulary.

VARIATION
Ask the learners to provide not just one vocabulary example, but as many as possible for each category.

6.6

LEVEL
Any

FOCUS
Pronunciation as a cue for recalling and categorising vocabulary items

MATERIALS
None

TIME
Variable

RATIONALE

Part of knowing a word is knowing how to pronounce it. The process of learning vocabulary involves the establishing of many different associations. The evidence of slips of the tongue suggests that, at least for native speakers of English, stress patterns are one principle by which words are associated with each other. There is also evidence that knowing a word's stress pattern makes it easier to recall that word in certain circumstances.

6.7

LEVEL
Elementary +

FOCUS
Stress variations according to the position of a word in a phrase

MATERIALS
List of phrases – see *Preparation*

TIME
15 minutes +

MOVING STRESS IN PHRASES

Part of knowing a word is knowing which syllable to stress. But this is not always consistent. Compare these two phrases (underlining indicates stressed syllables): <u>Au</u>gust the four<u>teenth</u>; the <u>four</u>teenth of <u>Au</u>gust.

Preparation

1 You need a list of phrases which illustrate the kind of dual behaviour of words exemplified above. You will find examples in the learners' speech, in your teaching materials, and simply by listening attentively to English. Here are a few examples:

an <u>inter</u>national <u>con</u>ference
the <u>con</u>ference was very inter<u>na</u>tional
<u>con</u>tinental <u>break</u>fast
<u>Eng</u>lish or conti<u>nen</u>tal?
<u>Good</u>bye to Ber<u>lin</u>
the <u>Ber</u>lin <u>Wall</u>
an <u>e</u>conomic re<u>co</u>very
the <u>rea</u>sons are eco<u>nom</u>ic
<u>death</u> in the after<u>noon</u>
<u>after</u>noon <u>tea</u>

2 Write a list of all the key words you are going to use, together with the two contrasting contexts for each (as above, but without any underlining or other markings) and photocopy it. Alternatively, you can dictate the phrases at the beginning of the activity.

Procedure

1 Distribute the photocopies or dictate the phrases.
2 Tell the class you are going to say them one by one, and they should listen and mark where the stress is in each occurrence of each key word by underlining the stressed syllable. Show them an example on the board first. It might be handy for them to use pencils, in case they need to change their minds.

3 Let them compare with each other and you, then read the phrases again so that they can check their results. Make sure you don't change the way you stress the phrases!

STRESS IN COMPOUNDS/TWO-WORD EXPRESSIONS

6.8

LEVEL
Beginner +

FOCUS
Stress patterns in compounds and two-/multi-word expressions

MATERIALS
One worksheet per learner or pair of learners (see example below)

TIME
10–20 minutes

You can use this type of exercise to sensitise learners to the notion of stress in compounds and two-/multi-word expressions, and to enable them to perceive patterns that may eventually help their own production.

Procedure

1 Give each learner a list of compounds or two-word expressions that are *noun + noun* and *adjective + noun* (e.g. *car ferry; hot water; fresh bread; pocket watch*).
2 Read the list out loud and ask the learners to mark the syllable where the overall prominence is placed.
3 Ask the learners if they can perceive any pattern, i.e. in noun + noun compounds, the stress has a tendency to fall on the first element, while in adjective + noun compounds, the stress has a tendency to fall on the second element. Point out, with examples, that these generalisations can vary with contrast, e.g. 'I asked for <u>hot</u> water, not <u>cold</u> water'.
4 Give the learners two columns of jumbled halves of compounds. Ask them to work in pairs or small groups and form compounds using one word from the first column and one word from the second until all the words have been used.

Example worksheet

wind	water
hot	well
red	paper
oil	tray
blue	flake
new	mill
white	potato
tissue	tape
snow	wine
ash	moon

© Longman Group UK Ltd 1992

5 Check that the compounds are correct. There may be several possibilities and this can give scope for further discussion.
6 Ask the learners (again working in groups) to divide the compounds into two groups according to their stress pattern.

CHAPTER 7

Tone groups, rhythm and intonation

7.1

LEVEL
Elementary +

FOCUS
The function of
tonic prominence

MATERIALS
A worksheet (see
example below)

TIME
10–20 minutes

TONIC PROMINENCE RECOGNITION EXERCISE

This activity can be used to sensitise learners to the relationship between emphatic stress and meaning. It can form part of a longer lesson devoted to listening (task: marking the stressed syllables in a stream of authentic speech, e.g. from the radio news headlines) and production (see 7.2 *Tonic prominence production exercise*). You can also link it to the practice of a particular grammatical structure, by including the structure (e.g. the present perfect tense) in each of the example sentences.

Preparation

Make a list of example sentences and a list of the possible meanings conveyed by each sentence. Produce a worksheet (see example below).

Procedure

1 Give learners a list of up to ten sets of multiple-choice answers. For example:

  1 a) he didn't
      b) not this Tuesday
      c) not Manchester √
  2 a) not tea
      b) not white coffee
      c) four not three

2 Check that the learners understand the meaning of the possible answers. The answers should be as simple in form as possible so as not to distract from the main aim of the activity.
3 Read out a list of up to ten sentences. Read at a natural speed but with sufficient time between each sentence for the learners to choose the correct answer. Make sure that you place the stress on only one part of each sentence so that only one of the answers is possible.

Example sentences (corresponding to the answers given above)

1 She went to <u>London</u> last Tuesday.
2 He had four cups of strong black coffee.

4 At the end of the listening stage, check the answers and, if necessary, repeat any sentences that have caused problems.

TONIC PROMINENCE PRODUCTION EXERCISE

You can use this exercise as a means of giving learners practice in relating emphatic stress to meaning and in producing stress patterns appropriate to the intended meaning. You can also use it as a follow-up to the *Tonic prominence recognition exercise* (7.1).

Preparation

You will need a list of up to ten sentences and a list of responses. These could be either on a handout or on the board or OHP. See examples below.

Procedure

1 Give or show your learners the list of ten sentences. For example:

She arrived on the early morning train from Manchester.

2 Give the learners a list of several possible responses to each sentence. For example:

... not the plane.
... not Newcastle.

3 Then, in open class, say one of the responses as a cue for each example sentence. Ask the learners (you may nominate a particular learner or wait for one to volunteer) to produce the correct sentence from the list with the tonic prominence in a place appropriate to the cue. For example:

Teacher: ...not the plane.
Learner: She arrived on the early morning <u>train</u> from Manchester.

Several different examples of tonic prominence can be obtained from the same sentence by giving different response cues for it.

4 After a number of examples in open class, the learners can then do the exercise in pairs or small groups, taking it in turns to play the role of cue-giver. Your role then is to monitor the progress of each pair or group and give help when required.

7.2

LEVEL
Elementary +

FOCUS
Placing tonic prominence according to intended meaning

MATERIALS
Handout with sentences and different possible meanings (see below for example)

TIME
10–25 minutes

EXTENSION

Give the learners a further list of sentences and encourage them to experiment with tonic prominence by placing it on different elements of the sentences and then suggesting potential meanings and responses themselves. This can be particularly successful as a group problem-solving activity.

Example sentences and response cues

1 She arrived on the early morning train from Manchester.
She didn't leave ...; ... not late; ... not evening; ... not plane; ... not Newcastle.
2 I asked you to buy me a bunch of red roses.
... not steal them; ... not just one; ... not yellow ones; ... not tulips.
3 She wanted me to paint the kitchen green.
... not him; ... not to paper it; ... not the bathroom; ... not pink.
4 He told John to ask a policeman the quickest way to the bank.
... not Peter; ... not to tell him; ... not a postman; ... not the cinema.
5 We went to Majorca on holiday last year.
We did, not them; ... not Corfu; ... not on business; ... not this year.

7.3

LEVEL
Elementary +

FOCUS
Contrastive
intonation
(especially the
fall–rise)

MATERIALS
None

TIME
20–30 minutes

TWENTY QUESTIONS TO A DRAWING

This is a sort of combination of 'Twenty Questions' and picture dictation. It presupposes at least some familiarity with prepositions. Traditionally, the limit for this type of guessing game is twenty questions, but you can vary this.

Preparation

On the basis of other learning priorities, decide on a number of items to form the contents of a picture. For instance, if you want the class to practise vocabulary concerning room furnishings, you might choose a sofa, an armchair, a stool, a vase, a clock, a rug, a table, a mirror, a potted plant, a lamp, a fruitbowl and possibly more.

Procedure

1 Ask each learner to produce – individually and secretly – a drawing which must contain the given items but in a freely chosen arrangement. Everyone should introduce some element of the unusual (e.g. the clock could be under the table). Make a drawing yourself, too.
2 The class put their drawings safely aside for the time being, and ask you yes/no questions about the positions of the items in your drawing in order to be able to draw a copy of it. If the answer is yes, just say so:

'Is the plant on the table?' – 'Yes'.

But if not, give an answer with this type of structure:

'No, the plant's on the floor.'
'No, the clock's on the table.'
'No, the plant's next to the table.'

Draw learners' attention to the form and intonation of your responses. It may well help to put example exchanges like the ones above on the board for reference. Get them to practise the intonation of these examples if necessary.

3 They are now ready to work in pairs and do the same exercise. Depending on how familiar they are with the use of the fall–rise (⟶ ⟋), you might need to circulate and give quite a lot of help with this.

NOTE

Intonation can be indicated on the board by drawing arrows that follow the movement of pitch, as above. You can also indicate intonation with arching sweeps of a hand or an emphasis pointer.

RATIONALE

This activity isolates a tendency in the native speaker's intonation system for a falling tone to be used for content which is presented as new, and a fall–rise to be used for content which is, although still important, presented as already in circulation or shared between speaker and listener. In the latter instance, many learners of English tend to use a simple rising tone instead of a fall–rise, and this can give an impression of over-dominance.

I DO

7.4

In real communication, distribution of tonic prominence is not fixed according to preexisting abstract principles, but varies according to the speaker's perception of how what they are saying relates to the ongoing discourse. This exercise works on developing awareness of and skill in using this principle, by taking as its domain a limited set of possible discourse conditions.

LEVEL
Elementary +

FOCUS
Assigning tonic prominence according to discourse conditions

Preparation

1 Choose a simple proposition which you know is true for some of the members of the class but not for others. Here, the proposition 'I live in Paris' is taken as an example.

2 If necessary, teach the forms *I do, I don't, so do I, neither/nor do I.*

MATERIALS
None

TIME
5–10 minutes

Procedure

1 Tell the class that this activity is going to involve each person in the room speaking in turn. You will start by making a true statement about yourself. Each learner in turn must confirm or deny that statement for themselves, but selecting only from the responses 'I do', 'I don't', 'so do I', 'neither/nor do I'.

2 In the early stages of the activity you may need to indicate who is to speak next, but ideally the turn should pass smoothly around the room until everybody has spoken. A possible sequence might be as follows (underlining indicates stressed syllables):

Teacher: I live in Paris.
Learner 1: So do I.
L2: So do I.
L3: I don't.
L4: I do.
L5: So do I.
L6: I don't.
L7: Neither do I.
And so on.

3 If you feel that the stressed syllables are not being sufficiently emphasised, point this out and start a second round, either in the same order as before or, for variety, going round the room in a different direction.

4 Repeat the exercise using different starting sentences which will generate practice of different auxiliary verbs. For example, 'I've been to England', 'I can type', 'If I was a teenager now, I'd choose to study English'.

5 Learners propose their own starting sentences.

7.5

LEVEL
Elementary +

FOCUS
Assigning tonic prominence according to discourse conditions

MATERIALS
None

TIME
5 minutes +

CORRECT THE TEACHER

Some learners may have waited a long time to turn the tables and correct the teacher. This is an opportunity for them to do so and also to practise an important aspect of pronunciation at the same time.

Procedure

Invite the learners to dictate numbers, which you will write on the board. Make deliberate mistakes, and correct them only when the learner who said the number (or another one) has shouted out a verbal correction with appropriate placement of tonic prominence. For example:

a)   Learner: Thirty five.
     Teacher writes '39'
     L: No, thirty five.

b)   L: Five hundred and eighteen.
     Teacher writes '519'
     L: No, five hundred and <u>eigh</u>teen.
     Teacher writes '580'
     L: No, five hundred and eigh<u>teen</u>.

EXTENSION

Learners do the same exercise in pairs, or as a whole class with a volunteer making the deliberate mistakes.

VARIATIONS

1 Instead of numbers, use dates (e.g. *Twenty first of January/Thirty first of January, Tenth of September/Tenth of November*), or playing cards (e.g. L asks for the king of hearts, T gives the queen of hearts, L says 'No, the <u>king</u> of hearts.') or any other set of items with similar contrasts.

2 Tell a known story with deliberate mistakes, which the class have to correct. For example:

   T: Little Red Riding Hood lived in a cottage in the middle of a desert.
   L: No, she lived in the middle of a <u>wood</u>.
   T: Oh, yes. She lived near a wood.
   L: No, <u>in</u> a wood.
   And so on.

CREATE YOUR OWN VERSE FORM

7.6

Through their experience of songs and rhymes, most people are aware of the principle of regular structures of rhyme and rhythm. (The limerick is one such structure well-known in the English-speaking world.) Here is an opportunity for the learners to create their own such structures (possibly drawing on models from their own cultures).

LEVEL
Lower intermediate +

FOCUS
Rhythmic structures

Procedure

MATERIALS
None

1 Tell the learners they are going to invent their own verse structure. You can specify a number of lines; it probably shouldn't be more than about six.

TIME
30 minutes

2 Ask them to produce a plan of the structure – line length, rhythm, stressed beats, rhyme, etc. – and an example of the genre (e.g. limerick).

3 They then swap their plans and compose samples of each others' genres.

4 Forms which catch on may become a vehicle for any written activity, such as an ongoing exchange of messages within the class, or a response to world events, or practice of language items introduced during the course.

7.7

LEVEL
Any

FOCUS
Rhythm and compression of unstressed syllables

MATERIALS
A metronome;
Optionally, lists of words on a handout

TIME
10 minutes

METRONOME

Preparation

You need a list of words and phrases with variable numbers of syllables and variable stress. Suitable examples include:

- lists of cardinal numbers
- train announcements, e.g:

   Calling at Stevenage, Peterborough, Grantham, Newark, Retford, Doncaster, Wakefield and Leeds.

- shopping lists, e.g:

   bread, carrots, milk, potatoes, apples, muesli, tea, tomatoes.

Procedure

1 Set the metronome going at a moderate speed and get the class to practise fitting individual items to the rhythm, with the stress falling on the metronome beat.
2 Get them to practise reading the whole list to the beat.
3 Reset the metronome to a faster, more natural speed and repeat the practice.

RATIONALE
Once the metronome is set at a certain speed, it will carry on relentlessly for ever. It gives a consistent rhythm to practise against, which cannot be guaranteed by tapping or clapping, for instance. At the same time, because the speed is adjustable, you, or the learners themselves, can control the difficulty of the task by choosing a suitable speed setting.

SHADOWING

Reading out loud is an activity requested by many learners but discouraged by teachers who feel that it has no real purpose and only gives practice in hesitant, inaccurate pronunciation. Here is a way of using the principle of reading out loud for more directed work on pronunciation.

Preparation

You need a piece of spoken English (one speaker) on tape. It could be something the class have already used for some other purpose. In any case, it should be something they have no trouble understanding. It is very important that it should be natural, unscripted, conversational English, which makes most published EFL pronunciation or listening material unsuitable. You also need a copy of the tapescript for everyone in the class.

Procedure

1 Play a short section of the tape – one sentence, or even less.
2 Leave a few moments silence to allow the sound of the words to register in the learners' ears.
3 Invite them to replay internally, without speaking, what they heard.
4 Replay the same section of the tape.
5 Repeat steps 2 and 3.
6 Now invite the learners to speak the same words in exactly the same way, and at the same speed. They can do this either one by one to the class, or all at the same time to themselves or to a partner. Let them try this a few times.
7 Replay the tape and let the learners evaluate their own performance. They may be able to identify discrepancies, or they may need the help of other people, including you, to pin them down. Discrepancies may involve sounds, connected sound sequences, word stress, speed, rhythm, segmentation, pausing, tonic prominence position or pitch movement (melody). Focusing on what seem to be the most important and most improvable of these, help them to come as close to the taped model as they can.
8 Now set them the challenge of speaking along with the voice on the tape, so that everyone's voice is in perfect unison with the tape. (This is 'shadowing'.) It will probably help to demonstrate this yourself. Depending on the size of the class, either get everybody to speak together, or split the practice.
9 Give them further opportunities to shadow the voice on the tape, until it seems their performance is as good as it can be for the time being.
10 Move on to the next short section of the tape and repeat the above procedure.

7.8

LEVEL
Elementary +

FOCUS
All aspects of pronunciation

MATERIALS
Tape recorder and recording (see below); Transcript of the recording; Optionally, a language laboratory

TIME
5–20 minutes

11 Go back to the beginning of the tape and get the class to shadow the first and second sections.

12 Add further sections and repeat the procedure for as long as it seems productive.

VARIATIONS

1 If you have the use of a language lab, record the spoken passage onto the learners' tapes and let them work at this exercise individually, at their own speed, recording their performance on top of the model when they feel ready, so that both tracks can be heard simultaneously. (It will still help, though, to introduce the activity and run through it briefly in non-lab mode.) Listen in and give individual help as necessary.

2 Record the passage onto individual tapes for each learner (most easily done in a language lab) and hand these over for the learners to practise shadowing with in their own time and space.

7.9

LEVEL
Elementary +

FOCUS
Awareness of body language as a way into stress and rhythm

MATERIALS
A video extract (See *Preparation*)

TIME
5 minutes +

VIDEO VIEWING

Preparation

Find a video extract in which someone is seen underlining the rhythm of their speech with hand gestures, nods of the head, etc. Sometimes you can find sections of quite a few seconds where the speaker maintains a perfectly regular rhythm with such gestures.

Procedure

1 Play the extract with the sound off.

2 Repeat this and ask the class to join in and imitate the body language of the speaker.

3 Play the extract as many times as necessary for them to do this pretty accurately.

4 If it seems possible from the context, invite the learners to guess what the speaker is saying.

5 Play the extract with sound, establish what is being said, and get the learners to imitate the speaker's body language again, this time adding the speech. Practise as necessary.

RATIONALE

We do not only speak with our mouths. One view is that body language acts as a kind of support to words. This exercise is based on the opposite premise; body language can form a basis on which to superimpose words.

PRONUNCIATION ROLE PLAY

This is particularly suitable as a warmer before a larger-scale activity, but has its own independent justification too.

Preparation

2.3 *Comparing sounds* and 2.4 *Bilingual minimal pairs* could provide useful preliminary work for this exploration of pronunciation differences.

Procedure

1 Tell the learners to work in pairs or small groups and to imitate or take the role of English speakers speaking English. Ask them what they need to do with their speech organs in order to do this which is different from what they usually do. Switching backwards and forwards between the two types of articulation may be helpful here in providing the key to the adjustments which need to be made in order to pronounce English well.
2 Next, tell them to imitate particular native speakers such as internationally well-known figures, landladies (in the case of those learners studying in Britain), other teachers, etc. speaking English. (It might help some learners to imagine they are representing these people on stage or in a film.) Again, ask them what adjustments they make in order to achieve this (or to approximate to it; the aim is not perfect mimicry).

7.10

LEVEL
Elementary +

FOCUS
Differences between the pronunciation of English and that of the mother tongue above the level of individual sounds

MATERIALS
None

TIME
5 minutes +

CHAPTER 8

Trouble shooting

8.1 PROBLEMS WITH /w/

Many learners find it difficult to pronounce the phoneme /w/, particularly in initial position as in *would* or *woman*. One solution here is to treat /w/ as a combination of the two vowel sounds /uː/ and /ə/, and to ask the learners to pronounce each in turn, gradually increasing the speed until they arrive at a sound that is very close to /w/, if not /w/ itself. Focus particularly on the rounded lip position at the beginning of the sound. The same principle can be applied to /w/ in context. Ask the learners to say the phonemes /uː/, /ə/ and /d/ in turn, once again gradually increasing the speed and arriving at *would*.

8.2 /w/ FOR /v/

Some learners regularly confuse /w/ and /v/, producing, for example, '*w*ery' instead of 'very'. One solution is to ask them to bite (gently!) their lower lip with the upper teeth before pronouncing the /v/ sound. This should ensure that there is no lip rounding and that 'very' is produced rather than '*w*ery'.

8.3 /f/ /p/ CONFUSION

In some languages, /f/ and /p/ are not separate phonemes, but simply variations (allophones) of the same phoneme. Thus speakers of these languages may find it difficult to distinguish between /f/ and /p/ aurally and will probably find it difficult to produce /p/, realising it as a strongly aspirated sound very close to /f/ but with minimal contact between the upper teeth and the bottom lip. In such cases, it will probably be necessary to work on the production of both /f/ and /p/. For /f/, the remedy shown above, i.e. biting the lower lip with the upper teeth, may well prove effective. /p/ can be realised more effectively by asking the learners to purse their lips tightly as if suppressing a laugh and to hold the air for a few seconds. Then ask them to release it as if it were an explosion. Repeat the exercise several times. If nothing else, it should at least be fun!

INSERTION OF /e/ BEFORE CONSONANT CLUSTERS   8.4

A common error for Spanish learners, for example, is to insert an extra sound before consonant clusters such as *st* and *sp* in initial position. Thus *Spain* is realised as '*e*spain' and *student* as '*e*student'. One remedy is to work on linking the last sound of the preceding word to the initial /s/ of the cluster. Thus, in the sentence 'I live in Spain', you can ask learners to say 'ins' followed by 'pain'. Although this will sound somewhat odd at first, the speed can gradually be increased and the result should approximate the desired pronunciation and remove the intrusive vowel sound. Another possible remedy is to ask the learners to produce /s/ in isolation (hissing like a snake!) and then to add, for example, 'pain', 'tudent', etc.

/p/ /b/ CONFUSION   8.5

Arabic speakers, among others, often confuse these two phonemes as they are not separate phonemes in their own language, but are variations of the same phoneme, which tends to be voiced with very little aspiration present. Thus, a typical error is something that may sound like '*B*eter's *b*laying *b*ing-*b*ong' for 'Peter's playing ping-pong'. The problem seems to lie in the absence of an explosion of air when trying to pronounce /p/. One solution is to ask learners to puff hard when pronouncing, for example, 'play'. A sheet of paper can also be used to demonstrate the importance of the amount of air expelled (see page 14).

/j/ PRONOUNCED AS /dʒ/   8.6

This is a problem frequent among Spanish speakers, particularly when confronted by the letter *y* in initial position. So *yes* is realised as '*j*ess', for example. One possible solution is to ask learners to think of the initial sound as /iː/ and to work actively on this with particular attention to lip position (i.e. spread). Ask your learners to begin by pronouncing /iː/ with spread lips and to hold this sound for a few seconds before adding /es/. Get them to do this several times, each time shortening the length of the initial /iː/ sound until they have a satisfactory /jes/. You may also need to work on this in context, as they may easily revert to /dʒ/ when trying to say 'Oh, yes', for example. The procedure outlined above should work here too, so something like /əʊwiːjes/ will be produced initially and this can gradually be speeded up to produce an accurate 'Oh, yes'.

8.7 INITIAL /h/

There may be several problems associated with the pronunciation of /h/. In some cases, it may be omitted from words such as 'house', 'help' and 'hope'. In others, it may be included unnecessarily at the beginning of words such as *egg*, *old* and *ate* (see 8.8 *Intrusive /h/*). Some learners may also use too much friction, articulating from the uvula rather than the glottis when pronouncing /h/ and thus producing a harsher /x/ sound, similar to the *ch* in 'loch'.

A possible remedy you could try in the first case is to ask the learners to whisper some words beginning with /h/ (see 3.4 */h/ through whispering* for further details), as the very act of whispering will require a certain amount of aspiration. Ask the learners if they notice the extra release of air as they whisper the initial /h/. This, at the very least, should make them aware that they *can* produce this sound! Now ask them to pronounce /h/ in context by giving them a number of words containing initial /h/. Tell them to begin by whispering the words and then gradually to get louder and louder. Some practice in context, i.e. using the words in a sentence, may also be necessary.

Softening /x/ to /h/ can be more problematic. One possible solution you can try is to ask your learners to puff a /h/ sound using as much air as possible.

8.8 INTRUSIVE /h/

In order to help with the intrusive /h/ problem, for example /hɜːθ/ for /ɜːθ/, you can work on the liaison between words. In the case of *earth*, for example, this will generally occur with the definite article preceding it and pronounced /ðiː/. Thus *the earth* will be realised as /ðiːjɜːθ/. If you yourself exaggerate the /j/ sound, the learners will probably focus on the production of this sound and the intrusive /h/ will be dropped.

When /h/ intrudes onto a word beginning with a vowel and that word is not preceded by another word, try to get learners to replace the /h/ with a glottal stop (i.e. /ʔ/). For example, if learners pronounce *it* as 'hit', ask them to say /ʔit/. You can get them to notice how to form /ʔ/ by having them imitate a machine gun as in /ʔiʔiʔi/.

8.9 PROBLEMS WITH /θ/ AND /ð/

This is a frequent problem for speakers of many languages. The word *thing*, for example, may be pronounced as something like 'sing', 'ting' or 'zing'. There are a number of possible solutions. Working with the word *thing*, you can ask your learners to begin by pressing the tip of the tongue firmly against the back of the upper front teeth. This *may* help.

If it still does not work, then you can ask them to bite (gently!) the tip of their tongue as they begin to pronounce the word.

Another possibility is a traditional favourite; the 'wet finger'. Ask your learners to place their forefinger in front of their mouth (as if miming 'Be quiet'). They then lick their finger as they pronounce the first sound of the word *thing*, for example. Again there should be some light contact between the tip of the tongue and the teeth.

If all of this fails, then you can try asking your learners to say words from their own language that begin with /s/ and pronounce them with a lisp. If they can do this successfully, they can then go on to try words like *sing*, *sick*, etc. in the same way. This should produce something fairly close to /θɪŋ/ and /θɪk/. You can apply the same procedures to words containing the voiced equivalent /ð/.

DENTAL /t/ AND /d/   8.10

In many languages, the phonemes /t/ and /d/ are dental rather than alveolar, as they are in RP English. Thus /t/ and /d/ are pronounced with the tip of the tongue lightly touching the back of the upper teeth rather than making contact with the alveolar ridge behind the upper teeth. This has the effect of making /t/ and /d/ sound very soft, for example, as in the case of Spanish learners, producing a sound that is very like /ð/, with a tendency to sound like a fricative rather than a stop. One solution is simply to point out the place of articulation in English on a mouth diagram and say that the tongue touches the alveolar ridge rather than the teeth. Get your learners to try this with words like *tent*, *try*, *red*, etc.

INTRUSIVE /ə/ IN FINAL POSITION   8.11

An error typical of Italian speakers is to insert an extra vowel at the end of words ending in a consonant sound. This seems to be particularly prevalent after plurals ending in /s/, /z/ and /ɪz/. As these particular fricatives are relatively easy to hold for a certain amount of time, one way you can affect the pronunciation of learners with this particular tendency is to ask them to make the final fricative last for a few seconds. Of course, this will sound exaggerated and will perhaps overcompensate for the problem, but the usual effect is to make the intrusive sound disappear. Ask your learners to say *trees, please, watches, wants,* etc. and to hold the final fricative, making the sound gradually die away.

8.12   INCORRECT STRESS PATTERNS

Many learners will tend to transfer the word stress patterns of their mother tongue to English or will be confused by the inconsistency of stress placement in English (e.g. *pho*tograph, pho*to*grapher, photo-*graph*ic). Thus a oO pattern may be realised as Oo and vice versa, with 'in'tend' being pronounced as ''intend' and ''breakfast' as 'break'fast'. There are a number of possible solutions to such problems. One way is to make learners aware of the factors that make a syllable more accented or stressed than those around it. One such factor is muscle power, usually manifested as loudness. Thus the stressed syllable may be slightly *louder* than its unstressed neighbours. So, ask your learners to say ''breakfast' with the first syllable very loud (perhaps to an exaggerated extent) and the second one very quiet. It is very difficult to do this and still maintain the overall stress on the second syllable.

Another factor affecting accented or stressed syllables is pitch; they are normally at a slightly *higher* pitch than unstressed syllables. A useful aid here is to use a board diagram that clearly shows that the first syllable (in this case) is at a higher pitch than the second. For example: *break*
           fast

Another technique is to hum, tap or whistle the stress pattern, accentuating the higher pitch of the stressed syllable. Now ask your learners to repeat the word, beginning with the pitch fairly high on 'break' and with a lower pitch on the second syllable 'fast'. You can help by whistling, humming or tapping the pattern. Now get them to add the loudness factor, so that 'break' is both louder and higher than 'fast'.

Another characteristic of a stressed syllable is that it often contains a full vowel as opposed to a weaker vowel found in the unstressed syllables, such as /ə/, /ʊ/ or /ɪ/. This difference in vowel quality is often accompanied by a slight difference in length. Thus the stressed sylla-ble is slightly *longer* than the unstressed one. Once again, you can get your learners to practise this by exaggerating the length of the stressed syllable and making the unstressed one as short as possible. Now add the other two factors, volume and pitch, and get them to practise once again. Although the model may be somewhat exaggerated, there should be an effective contrast with what was said before and at least an approximation of a 'correct' model. In order to reinforce the effect of the application of these three features of a stressed syllable, you can also ask your learners to stress a familiar word (one to which they can apply a correct stress pattern) incorrectly (i.e. to make normally unstressed syllables louder, higher and longer) and to notice both how unusual this sounds and how difficult it is to do.

Glossary

affricate

A sound beginning as a **plosive** or stop and continuing as a **fricative**. /tʃ/ and /dʒ/ are the two examples in English.

alveolar

A sound articulated by contact between the tongue and the alveolar ridge (the small ridge immediately behind the upper front teeth). /t/ and /s/ are examples in English.

aspiration

The small puff of air that sometimes follows a sound. For example, in English *p* is aspirated in *pin*, but when preceded by /s/ (e.g. *spin*), it is unaspirated; there is no puff of air.

assimilation

The feature whereby a sound is affected by its environment, usually by the sound following it, but sometimes also by the sound preceding it. This may change the quality of the sound in question (e.g. **voiced** to voiceless) or it may cause it to disappear completely. For example, the 'd' in *Good morning* in rapid speech may be articulated as 'Goo*b* morning' as the /d/ stop becomes a **bilabial** /b/ stop in anticipation of the bilabial /m/ which follows.

bilabial

A sound involving the use of both the upper and lower lip in its production. /m/ and /p/ are examples.

dental

A sound produced by contact between the tongue and the teeth. /θ/ and /ð/ are examples.

diphthong

A glide from one vowel to another. English has eight diphthongs with phonemic value; three closing to /ɪ/, namely /eɪ/, /aɪ/ and /ɔɪ/; two closing to /ʊ/, namely /aʊ/ and /əʊ/; and three centring to /ə/, namely /eə/, /ɪə/ and /ʊə/.

elision

The dropping of a sound altogether when it is affected by the following sound (see **assimilation**).

emphatic stress

The speaker may choose to emphasise a particular syllable or word for effect or to contrast it with another syllable or word. For example: 'She went to <u>Lon</u>don last week' (i.e. not Paris); 'She went to London <u>last</u> week' (i.e. not this week).

fricative

A sound articulated with accompanying friction caused by two of the articulatory organs (e.g. tongue and alveolar ridge) coming into close contact but allowing a restricted passage of air to pass through. Examples are /f/ and /s/.

front and back vowels

This refers to whether the tongue is raised towards the front of the mouth in the production of a particular vowel (e.g. /iː/) or towards the back (e.g. /ɔː/).

glottal stop

A closing of the glottis, as in the case of the first 't' in *right train* for example. The glottal stop is represented by the symbol /ʔ/. It is a common feature of English and is particularly noticeable in the Cockney pronunciation of 't' sounds in words such as *letter* and *bottle*.

homophone

A word pronounced in the same way as another but having a different spelling. *Bear* and *bare* are examples of homophones.

labio-dental

A sound involving the use of the lower lip and upper teeth in its production. /f/ and /v/ are the two examples in English.

lateral

A sound that involves air passing down the sides of the tongue as the latter comes into contact with the palate. /l/ is an example in English.

nasal

A sound whose production involves use of the nasal cavity (e.g. /m/).

open and closed vowels

/æ/, /ʌ/, /ɑː/ and /ɒ/ are open vowels, for example. The jaw position is, broadly speaking, open for the production of these vowels. The closed vowels, on the other hand, like /iː/, /ɪ/, /ʊ/ and /uː/ are produced with the jaw in a relatively closed position.

palatal

A sound that is produced by contact between the tongue and the hard palate (e.g. /j/).

palato-alveolar

A sound which is produced by contact between the tongue and the alveolar ridge with accompanying contact between the main body of the tongue and the palate. /ʃ/ and /ʒ/ are examples.

phoneme

The smallest element of meaning-changing sound in a given language. For example, we have the three phonemes /p/, /æ/, /t/ in the word *pat*. When one phoneme is replaced by a different one, e.g. /p/ by /b/, we have a new word – *bat*.

phonemics

The study of **phonemes**.

phonetics

The study of all human speech sounds.

phonology

The study of the sound system of a given language, including its sounds, stress patterns and intonation features.

plosive

A sound that involves contact between two of the articulatory organs completely blocking the air flow for an instant (otherwise known as a 'stop') and then releasing it in an 'explosion'. Examples are /p/ and /t/.

schwa

The /ə/ sound.

syllabic consonant

Certain consonants (/r/, /n/, /m/ and /l/) have vowel quality in certain positions, particularly in final position. Thus 'open' is rendered as /əʊpn/, rather than /əʊpən/.

tone group

A group of syllables containing a glide in pitch.

tonic prominence

The placement of stress in discourse by the speaker (often referred to as 'sentence stress').

tonic syllable

The syllable in any **tone group** where the glide in pitch begins.

velar

A sound produced by contact between the back of the tongue and the soft palate (e.g. /k/).

voiced consonants

These are consonants whose articulation is accompanied by vibration of the vocal cords (examples are /z/ and /g/ – compare with their voiceless equivalents /s/ and /k/). In the case of the stops (or **plosives**) /b/, /d/ and /g/, the onset of voicing occurs as the stop is released.

vowel reduction

The tendency of weak, unstressed vowels to reduce to /ʊ/, /ɪ/ and, particularly, /ə/.

Pronunciation table

symbol	key word	other common spellings	symbol	key word	other common spellings
consonants			**vowels**		
p	**pen**	ha**pp**y	iː	sheep	f**ie**ld t**ea**m k**ey** sc**e**ne am**oe**ba
b	**back**	ru**bb**er	ɪ	ship	sav**a**ge g**u**ilt s**y**stem w**o**men
t	**tea**	bu**tt**er walk**ed** dou**bt**	e	bed	**a**ny s**ai**d br**ea**d b**u**ry fr**ie**nd
d	**day**	la**dd**er calle**d** coul**d**	æ	bad	pl**ai**d l**au**gh (*AmE*) c**a**lf (*AmE*)
k	**key**	**c**ool so**cc**er lo**ck** s**ch**ool che**q**ue	ɑː	father	c**a**lm h**ea**rt l**au**gh (*BrE*)
g	**get**	bi**gg**er **gh**ost			b**o**ther (*AmE*)
tʃ	**cheer**	ma**tch** na**t**ure ques**t**ion **c**ello	ɒ	pot	w**a**tch c**ou**gh (*BrE*)
dʒ	**jump**	a**g**e e**dg**e sol**d**ier gra**d**ual			l**au**rel (*BrE*)
f	**fat**	co**ff**ee cou**gh** **ph**ysics hal**f**	ɔː	caught	b**a**ll b**oa**rd dr**aw** f**ou**r fl**oo**r
v	**view**	o**f** na**vv**y			c**ou**gh (*AmE*)
θ	**thing**		ʊ	put	w**oo**d w**o**lf c**ou**ld
ð	**then**		uː	boot	m**o**ve sh**oe** gr**ou**p fl**ew** bl**ue**
s	**soon**	**c**ity **p**sychology me**ss** **sc**ene			r**u**de
		li**st**en	ʌ	cut	s**o**me bl**oo**d d**oe**s
z	**zero**	wa**s** da**zz**le e**x**ample (/gz/)	ɜː	bird	b**ur**n f**er**n w**or**m **ear**n j**our**nal
ʃ	**fishing**	**s**ure sta**t**ion ten**s**ion vi**ci**ous	ə	cupboard	th**e** col**ou**r act**or** nati**o**n
		chevron			dang**er** **a**sleep
ʒ	**pleasure**	vi**s**ion rou**ge**	eɪ	make	pr**ay** pr**ey** st**ea**k v**ei**n g**au**ge
h	**hot**	**wh**ole	əʊ	note	s**oa**p s**ou**l gr**ow** s**ew** t**oe**
m	**sum**	ha**mm**er ca**l**m bo**mb**	aɪ	bite	p**ie** b**uy** tr**y** g**ui**de s**igh**
n	**sun**	fu**nn**y **k**now **g**naw	aʊ	now	sp**ou**t pl**ough**
ŋ	**sung**	si**n**k	ɔɪ	boy	p**oi**son l**aw**yer
l	**led**	ba**ll**oon batt**le**	ɪə	here	b**ee**r w**ei**r app**ea**r f**ie**rce
r	**red**	ma**rr**y **wr**iggle **rh**ubarb	eə	there	h**ai**r b**ea**r b**a**re th**ei**r pr**ay**er
j	**yet**	on**i**on **u**se n**ew** **Eu**rope	ʊə	poor	t**ou**r s**u**re
w	**wet**	**o**ne **wh**en **q**ueen (/kw/)	eɪə	player	
x	**loch**		əʊə	lower	
			aɪə	tire	
			aʊə	tower	
			ɔɪə	empl**oye**r	

Bibliography

Baker, A 1982 *Introducing English Pronunciation* CUP

Bradford, B 1988 *Intonation in Context* CUP

Brazil, D et al., 1980 *Discourse Intonation and Language Teaching* Longman

Brown, A 1991 *Pronunciation Models* Singapore University Press

Brown, A (ed.) 1991 *Teaching English Pronunciation: A Book of Readings* Routledge

Brown, A (ed.) forthcoming *Phon and Pron: Approaches to Pronunciation Teaching* British Council & Macmillan

Gimson, A 1980 *An Introduction to the Pronunciation of English* Arnold

Graham, C 1978 *Jazz Chants* OUP

Haycraft, B 1971 *The Teaching of Pronunciation* Longman

IATEFL *Speak Out!* The IATEFL Phonology Special Interest Group Newsletter

Kenworthy, J 1987 *Teaching English Pronunciation* Longman

Knowles, G 1987 *Patterns of Spoken English* Longman

Kreidler, C 1989 *The Pronunciation of English* Blackwell

Mortimer, C 1984 *Elements of Pronunciation* CUP

Poldauf, I 1984 *English Word Stress* Pergamon

Roach, P 1983 *English Phonetics and Phonology* CUP

Smith, B and Swan, M, 1987 *Learner English* CUP

Tench, P 1981 *Pronunciation Skills* Macmillan

Underhill, A forthcoming *Sound Foundations* Heinemann

Wells, J 1990 *Longman Pronunciation Dictionary* Longman